Drama Casebook

A Chronicle of Experience

John Challen

Lecturer in English Studies
Bishop Grosseteste College, Lincoln

METHUEN EDUCATIONAL LTD
London · Toronto · Sydney · Wellington

First published 1973 by Methuen Educational Ltd
11, New Fetter Lane, London EC4

© *1973   John Challen*

Printed in Great Britain by
Butler & Tanner Ltd, Frome and London
S B N   423   46900   2   (cased)
S B N   423   46910   X   (paperback)

Contents

Cover design based on a photograph by
Ron McCormick

Drama Casebook

Introduction

This book is a chronicle of experiences, with commentary. When one starts to talk or to write about Drama it is very easy to become tied down with definitions, confused by clashes of theories, over-involved in differences in emphasis or priorities. Furthermore, Drama tends to be the one subject of all on the curriculum most likely to be influenced by subjective considerations, and an approach which proves to be most exciting and fruitful with one teacher can well be a sufficiently resounding failure with another to justify his righteous 'I told you so!'

The status of Drama in schools varies considerably, too. In many, stimulating and fruitful work is being done with all pupils. In others, much good work is being done, but it is confined, sometimes to the younger children only, sometimes to those considered academically less able. The others have more serious matters to attend to. In some schools, sadly, Drama, is allowed to function rather like a donkey tramping round a primitive well, treading a carefully prescribed path and drawing forth the clear spring of inspirations exclusively for use in other fields: ten minutes at the end of a lesson can be used for doing a bit of a play on the subject which has just been studied, or for protracted collecting in of books and materials.

It can be argued that drama specialists do not always help. In a number of schools, it is a new and relatively strange subject and I have known staffs to be confused by jargon, by apparently irreconcilable differences between specialists in the subject, by the whole mystique which can be very confusing, and indeed alarming, to members of staff whose early conditioning may anyway lead them to believe that Drama is really nothing other than just playing round. If their view of the subject is further obscured by this mystique, this esoteric quality, these incomprehensible, to them, distinctions, they may well be inclined to dismiss the whole thing as a gimmick (or, worse, resignedly accept it as such, believing, as some teachers now feel obliged to, that gimmicks have to be indulged in if one is to appear progressive).

Drama is such an individual matter. Children, teachers, and situations vary so much. The views of specialists are not immutable either, for experience may well change these views. This has certainly been so with me. So, approaches vary from person to person, from situation to situation. It is damaging to disparage work because it does not suit one's own approach, for one may thus inhibit the chance of learning, and Drama is a subject in which one should be learning all the time. The learning may seem of little significance to others. It may even seem overwhelmingly obvious to someone else, but sometimes the obvious needs to be learned. As, for instance, when I once launched forty vital and ingenious young children in small groups, after nebulous preparation, on a dramatisation of 'Sir Eglamour'. I was astounded by the variety of activities the Knights and Dragons developed, by the uncharacteristic contributions of the Princesses, the downright noise, the alarming closeness to accidents, the sheer, purposeless fun of it all. They very soon forgot completely the starting point of the activity. Eventually, they wore themselves out, but it damaged my name in the school. Fortunately, it was a teaching practice, and students are fortunate in being able to leave the resolution of such problems to others.

When I started my teaching career, it was in a secondary technical school, with eighty pupils. Here, I felt that Drama was inappropriate except as an out-of-school activity. We had far more important things to attend to in lesson time, for the pupils were working towards 'O' levels. Everyone took English – that was readily acceptable because, for one thing, everybody needs to read and write, and for another, they also all needed an 'O' level in that subject. Drama came under Eng. Lit., and we were not taking that. I accepted without question that lesson time should be given up almost exclusively to the study of examination subjects, except for games – and I somehow accepted intuitively that it was entirely proper that this subject alone should occupy timetable without adding an 'O' to the pupils' qualifications. I am not saying that this acceptance was necessarily misguided (nowadays, when curriculum reform is so vigorous it is indeed unsafe to be dogmatic in rejecting any one approach since it could well be next term's new theory); but to accept without questioning is another matter. 'Because it is there' is arguably a sounder reason for climbing a mountain than for accepting one particular form of time-table or syllabus.

I did feel that Drama should be essentially enjoyable, and I also tended to the widespread view that education, like medicine, should be rather nasty if it was to do real good. I carried on my Drama in youth work – not in the lavishly equipped youth wings which one often sees nowadays attached to new schools, but in any part of the youth club hut which was not filled by table tennis, or darts, or football training. Generally, my groups contained a core of real enthusiasts supplemented by a few people who were persuaded into taking part either by the enthusiasts or, quite often, by the youth leader, who could generally employ subtle bribes or threats. The trouble with members so recruited was that they tended when bored to drift off temporarily, which was irritating, or permanently, which could be a major disaster if they did it just before a production. One such member tended not to turn up to productions if offended, so we had to be very tactful and subtly flattering. The enthusiasts were committed; the others, often feeling ill-at-ease and scared of being laughed at, found themselves almost inevitably taking the smaller, duller, less important parts which increased their sense of not belonging. Keeping everyone enthusiastic was impossible, and this took away some of the pleasure from the work.

The enthusiasts remained keen – generally. On one sad occasion, however, I thought that I would give our work added impetus by entering for the area Youth Drama Festival. The adjudicator was clinical, technical, dispassionate. The group tried to follow his analysis of our shortcomings in technique, but all they really understood was our position – last – and our total percentage, so low that it got a laugh, but not from us. Since then, I have been concerned with excellent youth drama festivals. In West Sussex we used for some years only adjudicators who knew and understood the difficulties of working with youth groups. They gave a brief adjudication immediately after the performances but kept their detailed analysis for the next day, during which all the competing teams came together for a one-day course. These were by far the most successful festivals I have come across. All the young people taking part enjoyed themselves, and surely it is a good thing if festivals live up to their name; otherwise they can be bitter, intense and unhappy affairs.

The type of festival including a one-day course certainly helped to give a feeling of involvement to the less dedicated members of youth drama, and it certainly increased their enjoyment. Of course, enjoyment is not the only thing. I also came to feel that it was important for Drama to extend the people involved in it. In amateur groups, you come across the person who enjoys himself, certainly, but by playing the same part over and over again. Having discovered one thing he can do, he does not attempt anything else. There is also the person who is always the maid and would dearly like to try something else, but doesn't ever get the chance.

I was fortunate in being able to join the staff of, and later direct, youth drama summer schools – annual weeks of work on Drama for enthusiasts. I found these most enjoyable, but after a while I found myself questioning what we did here. Generally we spent the week on producing three short plays, or equivalent excerpts from longer ones. Time was also given up to social events and to the production of a revue, primarily for our own entertainment. Here, there was no question of having to get hold of some reluctant table-tennis player to make up a cast; everyone was keen and dedicated. Yet quite a number of our students were under-employed, when I came to think about it. One year, one group did the play scene from *Hamlet*. Five or six of the group were relatively fully employed, but the courtiers certainly were not. Gradually, therefore, we widened the scope of the courses, giving the students the chance to write, improvise, experiment, work out lighting plots, help in making settings, costumes, and properties – and perhaps most important of all, to produce plays and scenes from plays themselves, as well as playing in other people's productions. In other words, we tried to give them the experience necessary to go off and initiate Drama work for themselves, which many of them did. I found myself questioning more of my presumptions. Previously, I had not really thought about giving young people any experience other than that of being in one of my productions – an experience not very different in kind from that already offered by most schools and youth clubs – yet one really only learns to produce by being given a chance to do it, which may well be why some areas have a shortage of producers but a superfluity of performers.

An occasion arrived when I found that a dialogue exercise at school had developed into a play and the children were keen to put it on. I could not think of a good reason why they should not, so we found two other plays to go with it and arranged to borrow a hall so that we could put them all on. I can still remember how nervous I felt about this enterprise. Somehow, 'putting on a play' seemed to me an awesome undertaking, a daring venture. I did not then realise that most parents are prepared to suffer quite a lot on behalf of their children. On the first night, I could not bring myself to give the order to open the curtains, and went away while a courageous boy took it upon himself to launch the venture. The plays were very successful. I felt that I had brought off something bold – and unique. Long after I had lost my reverence for my daring I still found the actual moment of ringing up on a production a daunting experience. Nevertheless, my first experience of Drama in schools was an exhilarating one, and made me feel important.

I decided that Drama might be an interesting subject to teach and moved to a large secondary modern boys' school as a specialist in the subject. I think I learned more there than at

5

any other time in my teaching career. Until then, I had taught only children who were motivated by the need to pass their exams, who had been selected by examinations – and who could be returned whence they came if they failed to measure up to the academic or disciplinary standards. From that I moved to a school where, in those days, only a small proportion of the pupils stayed to take exams, but many left as soon as they were able to do so. It was overcrowded, as many schools were at that time. Much of the accommodation consisted only of huts. The hall had a small stage, but it was fully used throughout the day – first for a crowded assembly, then for PE (with little apparatus), then for dinner, then again for PE. After school, it was often in use for badminton and other activities. There was very limited storage space under the stage, and that was once spectacularly flooded. The switchboard was rebuilt by two of the boys with considerable skill, but it could only take one dimmer, and when all the stage lights were in use, the whole area of the school, including the hall and workshops, was likely to black out without warning. This didn't worry the actors, who were used to it, but it caused unrest among the audiences.

Many of the classrooms were daunting, too. Apart from the workshops and the laboratory, which also served as a general subjects teaching area, there were no specialist rooms. Most class-rooms were filled – over-filled, for the classes were very large – with old, unattractive, unwieldy furniture. At the front stood a teacher's desk, and generally there was very little space in which to get to it.

The lack of space did not trouble me too much initially. At that time, Drama meant essentially scripted plays to me, and the school had a good stock of plays of varying appro-priateness. The stock of good readers was more limited and I found I was frequently having to snap 'Be quiet!' at the others while readers, generally the same ones each week, ploughed through the script and the rest of the class, sharing between, or among, themselves 'followed'. I felt hurt by the lack of enthusiasm of the less able, feeling that they of all groups should have most to gain from the subject. It was my first experience of teaching children who were not already motivated, by home pressures, by examination requirements, or by the status of the school. It was certainly my most valuable teaching experience and I would suggest that all teachers would stand to gain from spending at least some of their time in a school where physical or social conditions are difficult. For the first time I found myself having to cope with physical limitations and, more important, I had to catch the interest of the children if I wanted to enjoy my work – or even to avoid having a difficult time. I had to learn a lot (including some things about my own limitations) and to work much harder than I had done before.

I had to learn that children will not listen automatically simply because I am talking, or about to talk; to work to ensure that what I was saying or doing was sufficiently interesting to catch the attention and to retain it. I had to learn to accept initially what the children had to offer without looking down on it, and then to work to extend their range of achievement.

I did a lot of filming here; it was one way of overcoming the physical difficulties, but I discovered others. Even cumbersome desks could be moved, and the amount of space that could be found was surprising. Some classrooms had tables, and these could be stacked, not interlocking neatly as the newer purpose-built furniture does, but nevertheless with comparative safety. My tape-recorder was very useful, and we found that we could make 'radio' plays even in very cramped conditions. Small groups, I found, took up less space than large ones (however self-evident that may seem, it was experience which brought it home to me) and individuals could do mimes or solo acts in very little space indeed. Immovable furniture tended to be incorporated into the action, as a German bunker, a tower, part of a cliff, and so on. But the most important thing I learned here was that if I threw aside my preconceptions, worked to make the subject interesting instead of assuming that by some divine right it was, kept alert to see what things caught the children's enthusiasm and how to make the most of them, they enjoyed their Drama. They really looked forward to it, became far more co-operative not only in the lessons but at other times as well – even when I was on dinner duty – and my whole job became very much easier. Again, this is a truism, one of those self-evident statements which we automatically nod to almost from the first week of our training – but experience reinforces and illuminates even well-worn themes.

From this school, I went to a new comprehensive school, starting in a new town with three hundred first year children. The job attracted me very much – Head of the Speech and Drama Department which had three full-time members – though the projected size of the school worried me very much. Numbers were due to rise to 1,750, though in fact it not only passed that alarming number but 2,000 also, earning itself a place in the *Guinness Book of Records*. By this time, many of my preconceptions about the teaching of Drama had been modified, but I still held a full armoury of beliefs about the essential characteristics of large schools, and especially large comprehensive schools. That I came to modify these, too, is not really relevant in this context, except in that it further encouraged me to suspect that generalisations of any kind, especially when delivered or held with considerable confidence (and especially those which I hold or deliver), obscure realities rather than illuminate them. Most of this book is concerned with my experience at this school, first in charge of Speech and Drama and later as Head of Lower School, 800 first and second year children, but still teaching Drama and now able to relate it to a range of subjects. Obviously, one does not carry experience about in separate, non-spill compartments, and the other work I have referred to here has influenced me a great deal, so there is often reference, direct or implicit, to it.

In each section of the book I shall try to give a straightforward account of some aspect of work which took place, and then follow it with commentary. My aim is to emulate the higher class newspapers, and keep news and views separate. The comment, to clarify things still further, is set out differently from the account. This also has the advantage of relieving me from the tedious necessity of constantly reiterating 'I think', 'in my opinion', 'it seems to me', and so on. I shall try to keep account and comment as separate as possible, though there are occasions when the comment will be interpolated where this seems more appropriate than waiting till the end of a section.

It will be obvious that I am committed to a strongly held personal viewpoint on the central importance of Drama in education, and I hope that the experience I have outlined in this section, together with the more detailed accounts to follow, will show why I have come to hold this viewpoint. Too often, Drama is simply a frill tacked on to the straight hem of the real curriculum, external to the real life of the school. But, as I see it, Drama has a fundamental part to play in the life of a school, illuminating other subjects, developing imagination, verbal facility, confidence. Children should have regular time devoted to Drama work whatever the timetable situation – as much time as possible. And it goes without saying that I mean all children, not, for instance, just the first and second years in a secondary school – and especially not only the less able children. The gains in other subjects should be considerable, and the gains for the children themselves incalculable.

Properly used, Drama should produce the opposite of those characteristics which it is sometimes supposed to develop. It should produce not precociousness, but a direct and pleasing lack of self-consciousness; not selfishness or egotism, but the ability to work within the group, for the good of the group; not temperament, but steady craftmanship. And above all, it should produce an understanding of the right use of Drama, not as a means to show off oneself or one's talent, but as a means of sharing thoughts, ideas, sentiments.

Ultimately, the pupils should reach the stage where they themselves use Drama, not the depressingly common one in which they are used in Drama by their elders and betters. It is still frequently believed that it is only the teacher, or the youth leader, or the local adult producer, who has the sole key which will unlock the dramatic box of delights. And, of course, it is a bit galling for dynamic and possibly egocentric teachers like myself to find themselves reduced progressively from

B

prime mover and inspiration, to catalyst and encourager, to involved observer, to audience – or even to being offered a part (and not a very good one at that) in a joint student-staff project initiated and produced by pupils. But it is – small encouragement – a logical development. If Drama has developed in the way I feel it should, the pupil should be able to experience all aspects, not simply that of being allowed to be in the teacher's production, however good. And some are not even good.

After such a dogmatic series of assertions, you will readily understand why I have tried to divide up the subsequent sections on the pattern I have indicated: some experiences, followed by some comment. I have tried in the various sections to illustrate different aspects of the work, not to give a sequential account. However, I hope that an over-all picture will emerge. For simplicity, I refer to the subject as 'Drama', ennobling it with a capital D. I think it is too young – and too comprehensive – a subject in schools to be fragmented, even in terminology. So whether it is movement, or pure dance, or improvisation or speech, or happening, it has the same general title. On our timetable, after consideration, we had described the subject as 'Speech and Drama'. This became rapidly, 'S and D', then, irreverently, 'Spit and Dribble'. I don't think the title mattered much, anyway. The children understood what they were about.

Chapter 1

Lessons

Tuesday morning in the gym. Gradually, the children arrive –
thirty-four first year boys and girls, a full range of ability
through from the child who cannot as yet read with any degree
of fluency to the child who has all the advantages and already
shows considerable academic strengths. Some wear their PE
kit, some wear brightly coloured casual clothes. Some disguise
the fact that they have forgotten to bring anything to change
into by slipping football shirts on; these hang loosely over their
trousers. There is considerable competition for the ropes, which
have been got out by the first arrivals, and some squabbling
over whose turn it is to use one next. Other children take out
mats from the store and work on a variety of activities, one
simply repeating a tentative forward roll over and over again,
others developing complicated balancing acts. Some girls play
leap-frog, some boys practise basket-ball shots. The gym is
filled with the noise of enjoyment.

When everyone has arrived and had a chance to work off
excess energy, the activity is brought to an end. Mats and ropes
go away, for all the floor space is needed. The children all lie
down, the scufflings and fidgetings die away and the lesson has
begun. We do a number of standard exercises: they are puppets
and I work the strings. They come alive in various ways.
Sometimes they work in an abstract way, not tied to any
particular situation, simply animating the fingers, the hands,
the arms, and so on, bringing them to life, using them in different ways. Sometimes they come to life from relaxation through
an imagined situation, starting from floating on a lilo on a warm
summer's day. They enjoy this and seem absorbed in their work
and so I take a risk. Some of the boys are particularly lively and

have a keen sense of the ridiculous and I know that they tend to
think of moving to music as essentially a feminine activity to
which the standard response of any self-respecting male is a
giggle and an unflattering remark. I do not tell them that I now
want them to do someting beautiful or aesthetic, but I say that
I feel encouraged to try something more difficult with them.
This time they will come to life from relaxation with no guidance
but the music. The record player is already switched on, the
record is in place, ready for such an opportunity. I play the
record and the activity starts again from relaxation as before.
Some of it is really moving, but I do not comment. I do not wish
to break into their concentration on the music nor do I want
to make them feel that this work is being watched by anyone.
One or two of the boys glance round at first, self-conscious,
ready to giggle defensively if necessary, but nearly everyone is
concentrating on doing successfully something which is difficult.
The music, which started quietly, becomes stronger, more
assertive. The children, listening intently, respond immediately.
Before it lightens and becomes brisker and more perky, I
turn the volume down and thank the children. No comments
this time; they have enjoyed their success. The risk was worth
taking and next week I will try something different. One boy
has enjoyed himself enough to ask what the music was. *Billy
the Kid* – acceptable.

Some people have immediate success with movement
work, whether with boys or girls. Others struggle worthily
and steadily lose heart as the boys start playing about and
the girls sit down and 'can't think of anything'. Sometimes
this is because of a whole range of circumstances beyond their
control, and there is really very little point in struggling on in
an increasingly sour situation, battling with obstructive
children and achieving nothing but hostility towards the
teacher and the subject. Sometimes, though, the approach
can make all the difference – the balance between success
and failure is a nice one, and quite small things can affect
the outcome because, although apparently insignificant

themselves, they tend to make the children self-conscious or ill-at-ease. Having enough space is important. Perhaps a really good teacher with a co-operative class can produce exciting work in cramped conditions, but for someone who is making a tentative start, working in a hall – or, better, a gym which has, for boys, athletic connotations and is often a bit less open to casual passers-by – makes a difference. If children are constantly thumping into one another, they will inevitably become distracted and lose the quality of absorption which helps boys especially to lose self-consciousness. Wearing different clothes helps in two ways: whether the children are wearing casual clothing or activity clothing, what they are wearing has associations and helps to establish a particular atmosphere. Besides, a lot of children will very properly feel inhibited if asked to lie, leap or roll about in their standard school clothing – they know what their mothers will say when they get home. Certainly up to the end of the second year, and very possibly well after that, separating boys and girls does not necessarily help – indeed, it can limit the overall development of work because boys and girls have different, often complementary, qualities to contribute and both can learn from contact with a different approach.

A wide ability range is, similarly, most valuable; both for variety of approach, and because ability in Drama does not necessarily relate to IQ, reading age or social background. All kinds of children should be able to contribute usefully and gain pleasure and confidence from seeing their contributions considered with respect. There is a danger here of a sort of inverted liberalism: of course, one can feel, this is something that a less bright child *can* excel at, so he needs Drama more than the more able child. Certainly, in subjects where oracy is as important as, or more important than, literacy, the apparent difference between children of different ability ranges becomes less and less. But one of the great advantages of Drama work is that a group does not sub-divide itself into above average or below average children; each child has an individual and unique contribution to make. The advantage of an orally-based lesson is that each child can make this contribution, provided that academic inhibitions are not replaced by others.

Now a change of pace. The children leap about trying to tap (or thump) their partner's right knee without retaliation. After the sustained concentration and imaginative work the change is welcome. More energy is used up and the children settle to more static work in pairs – or threes, for a partnerless child in a community of partners is a sad sight. They do the 'mirror' work which I have used in Dance Drama (q.v.). It is easier done in pairs, but the threes use extra ingenuity and so gain extra satisfaction from their results. After work in pairs, we build a scene in which I narrate a story of prospecting for gold, wonderful wealth, snowstorms, perilous crossings of mountain ranges, narrow ledges, icy rivers. An unsophisticated and melodramatic story, but each child re-creates it in his own way as I tell it. This time, they are concentrating on the story and on translating it into action. Some perform only in mime, some speak, some make noises – not only for themselves but also for the wind or the surging water. They are not aware of each other – two children, inching across a narrow ledge hundreds of feet above a chasm do not notice each other as their ledges cross. At the end, they can either make their way to safety, or die. By far the greater number die in a picturesque range of ways.

When we are all safe, or dead, or near enough dead if we are spinning it out, we sit for quick instructions for some group work: 'before and after'. Each group will make two 'frozen' pictures, one supposedly taken before an event and the other after. The rest of us will deduce what has happened between the two. A torrent of questions – how big should the group be; should the pictures be still ones; do we have to do two; can we have seven in our group? – is interrupted by impatient moves by the others, who start work. So do the questioners, unanswered but contented. They will work it out for themselves. The groups do not need long to bring their ideas into shape. Most of them swirl into action immediately. A few do not; I do not immediately swoop on them with suggestions, for different groups work in different ways and some like to sit and consider for a while. It is tempting to stir everyone to a uniform pitch of activity; difficult to avoid feeling that unless one is involved with large sections of the work in progress one is somehow failing; unflattering to realise that it might well be a much better thing if that quarrelling group resolved its difficulties without outside intervention. Before long, all the groups are ready, except one. I make a quick estimate of the reason – perhaps they are as yet a bit hesitant about presenting work to a potentially critical group and need reassurance; perhaps they were just unlucky and their idea didn't work out; perhaps they want to be coaxed and made a fuss of. Different situations need different handling. This group wants to be coaxed. They are soon ready and, with the other groups, show their scenes. It is generally very easy to guess what is supposed to have happened between the two groupings, but that is not the real point of the exercise. We develop the discussion to consider the groupings themselves, admiring those which show enterprise, commenting on the ways the attention is focused, moving some of the group round to see if a better effect can be achieved. One group makes use of the wallbars and benches to make other levels which, it is generally agreed, is commendable. Comments are welcomed and come freely, but it is fully understood that they must be constructive.

Variety is important, combined with a sense of swift transition from one piece of work to another, to emphasise that this is precious time which must not be wasted. To help in the quick transitions and to avoid the general feeling of aimlessness which comes from waiting, please, for quiet and order, I tried from the beginning to establish with each group readily recognisable control patterns. When I wanted them to listen, I invariably said, 'Right. Will you listen, please?' and they soon became used to responding to this. Very often the instructions or advice would be quickly given and the activity would immediately start again, but when I had something lengthier to say, or when I particularly wanted them to concentrate on what I was saying or others were doing, then I sat them down. They soon became used to this signal. (Rather authoritarian in some views, as I have been told, but my concession to an easy life.) Of course, a lot depended on the way in which it was done. It is most unreasonable to stimulate children to an animated exchange of ideas and then nag them because they don't stop the moment you want them to.

But, as many students are frequently reminded, it is certainly easier to relax from a relatively tight control than to do the opposite. I have been sad at times to see teachers or students losing all confidence, rapport and sense of enjoyment as they struggle to re-establish an atmosphere in which they can work. It really is better to decide beforehand how one wishes to establish a quiet atmosphere when necessary than to snap and nag at the children, who quite possibly can't hear you anyway, and impose restrictions which they will almost inevitably resent.

A mixture of approaches – individual, small group, pairs, large group, whole class – helps to keep the work alive. Overlong concentration on one aspect turns it into a chore. Sharing the work with others is sometimes useful, but not always. It is tedious working with children who believe that anything they do in Drama is incomplete if it is not performed for others; but I do not believe that all Drama is a matter of private, personal creation which would be sullied by being shown to anyone else. An exercise like the one on grouping is particularly valuable if opened to discussion because it is a way for children to absorb technique without formal instruction. I have always found this sort of background knowledge of technique invaluable in productions, particularly in crowd scenes where they have understood what I was talking about without the need for lengthy technical exposition or rigid regimentation.

Our lesson has not, so far, contained much work involving speech and I now give an opportunity for this in group work.

Some children still prefer to work in mime, but others are interested in developing character and situations through the use of speech. I give the children a theme to work on. This time, I ask them to build a scene round a fall, or an accident. I have found that many of the children prefer to have such a suggested focus for their work, but I always take care to emphasise that they can work on any idea which has caught their interest, even if it does not fit in neatly with the suggested theme. I wander round the groups as they are working, commending points in each group's work, for they will not all be able to 'perform' as most of the seventy-minute period has been used up. I try to choose different groups this week from last, but I do not keep to any rigid system. I explain why I have asked each particular group to share its work with the rest: each group has some individual point of interest, a good story, piece of characterisation, dramatic moments, piece of movement – something. One can select a range, some talented, some rather hesitant about their standard.

The time is now officially up, but, as always, they want to do a bit more. We quickly run through one of their favourite crowd scenes – a market in a warm country which is later overwhelmed by an earthquake and a volcanic eruption. The scene starts with assurance, some children buying and selling, some lounging, some playing, some making things. The conversation grows and the action becomes increasingly animated. Suddenly, the disaster. The gym echoes with screams (anxious children hurry up from the changing rooms below). We have a wide variety of attenuated deaths: crushing by collapsed buildings, burning by ash or molten lava, asphyxiation. When everyone is dead, a moment's pause before they rush off to the changing rooms. They all enjoyed the last piece, which provided a loud and exciting finish, but it was obvious that they had done it fairly often – it was smooth, mechanical. I look at my half envelope which carries unobtrusive notes on ideas for use in the lessons. I have not developed one line I particularly wanted to, a purely physical exercise which we started in a previous lesson and which showed signs of developing well. However, this lesson is now at an end and it will have to wait until next week. An over-rigid adherence to a particular plan could have led to the inhibition of other interesting work.

Drama is not just speech, nor is it just movement; and children should become accustomed to choosing which medium, or combination of media, best suits what they wish to do. They learn from making the decision and putting it into practice. Of course, advice must be readily available, but it is the job of the Drama teacher to act as catalyst, and some reactions readily take place without one. The problem of selection is always difficult, whether of groups who are to show their work, or of children who are to take the major parts in some production. The best thing, especially with this age-range, is to emphasise at all times that there is so much of value on offer that being selected is necessarily a random business. Otherwise, some groups, some individuals, begin to look upon themselves as 'the best' and develop a belief in their own implicit superiority. This is not good for them nor for those with whom they come into contact. And indeed, the perceptive teacher can find much of value in the work of different groups – it is good that he should, for the constant selection of one type of 'best' could not only be bad for those selected but also lead to all groups doing the same work, reflecting what the teacher finds most immediately worthwhile. There is another danger. In repeating a piece of work too often it can become automatic, uninvolved, though of course there is a case to be made for having a few pieces of work which are familiar, undemanding, now rather featureless – like ancient dramatic teddy bears, certainly not for public display.

The lesson by no means covered the full range possible, but there is a lot to be said for flexibility. It is a good plan to have plenty of material available so that one does not have to press on inexorably with one idea which fails to come to life, simply because one does not have another with which to replace it. One piece of music might prove to be quite the wrong one for that particular situation or for those children. I always feel a small and possibly illogical feeling of disappointment when I see, say, a student making her way to a Drama lesson with only one record firmly held and obviously to be used, whatever the circumstances. I always like to take a pile in with me, giving a variety and somehow contributing to the feeling that lots of music is constantly and quite normally available. If one is limited to just one piece, the mood might not be right for it and it would be wrong to use it just because it was there. A scene which you had set your heart on developing might simply refuse to come to life. A beautiful moment might turn to laughter. Part of the trouble with Drama work – and especially the movement or dance aspects of it – is that those who initiate it may well feel intensely committed to what they are doing and their very intensity, their earnestness, may make the children uneasy. A common way of dispersing tension is with a good laugh.

II

Friday afternoon, the final seventy minutes of the day. The class assembles, again boys and girls, but this time a set of second year children all of approximately the same academic ability. A few of the thirty have changed, but the changing rooms are not available for them and not many care to use the inadequate space in cloakrooms and toilet areas. Nevertheless, an increasing number feel that being changed for the lesson has advantages which outweigh the drawbacks – particularly the older children. The room, which was designed as a canteen area, though far too small for its intended purpose, makes a large classroom area. It is square and two of its walls are filled with glass – window from floor to ceiling, looking out over grass into other classrooms which adjoin the same courtyard area. Chairs are the only furniture in the room, though there are portable blocks and steps available in the hall which adjoins the room. There is also a property and costume store in one of the adjoining areas, and there are a number of odd empty

19

spaces around in which groups of children can work if they wish. It is by no means an ideal area for Drama work, though when I see the conditions in which others work, and produce live, worthwhile results, I realise that I am lucky in many respects.

The great advantage of this particular area was uncluttered space, which is always of prime importance. Light, flexible equipment, screens, blocks, rostra, etc. would be most useful. So, too, would be simple but flexible lighting: a small portable switchboard, for instance, with facility for cross-plugging of dimmers, and easily portable and fixable lighting fitments; not necessarily the large, cumbersome and limiting things that are hung around a lot of school stages. I would happily accept mercury vapour lights which are becoming increasingly sophisticated. These could, of course, each have their own special dimming switch which would obviate the need for a central switchboard. For most efficient use of this equipment, the area should be capable of being blacked out. This would have the added advantage of cutting out external distractions; it can be most discouraging to reach a gratifying point of intensity and concentration in a lesson only to have it broken into by the sight of a group of passers-by pausing to gaze in and comment. This would be a reciprocal advantage, for it can be very distracting for a sober maths lesson to have to compete with animated Drama activity. For this reason, too, sound insulation is also important, but this does not mean that the Drama area should be isolated. On the contrary, it should be contiguous to other subject areas and available for children from them to move in for Drama-based work. An adjoining work area would be most useful with facilities for making things, painting, electrical work and so on. So, too, would be a large collection of properties and simple costumes, cloaks, hats, swords, etc. The shape and furnishings of the Drama area should not pre-empt the choice of method of presentation of work.

We have been working on the theme of Youth in Revolt, and this period is to be devoted to working out improvisations in groups. In fact, the degree of actual improvisation varies markedly from one group to another. Some have a flexible approach and their scene is changing all the time. This approach seems better suited to the flippant or fantastic treatment of a theme and this time, although they start seriously, their work becomes lighter and seriousness is soon dissolved in laughter. I take the point up with them: should they perhaps aim for greater variety and not finish so frequently with a flippant piece of work? Is it a good thing that an originally serious intention should finish in quirky humour? Is the neatness of the resolution of their situation, with a smart last line giving the feeling of a revue sketch, too facile? They consider these questions sensibly, but the ambience of this piece at any rate is too firmly established now and they cannot bring themselves to change. They have a flair for this sort of thing, and enjoy doing what they do well.

Others spend a long time discussing the theme and their treatment and story line. Slowly and steadily, discussing and improvising, considering, then changing some aspects of the improvisation, trying again, considering again, they proceed by practice and consideration of ideas to produce a scene which, though in fact not written down, nevertheless has a set script which, once established, varies very little in subsequent runs through. Others do write down some of the script, but this takes time and is not perhaps the most efficient way of going about this particular exercise, for if a script is written down then it still has to be memorised. One group tries to use a tape recorder but in this context they do not find it a very productive approach, though in some circumstances it can be very valuable.

Some groups concentrate primarily on a story line, some on the characters, some on particular episodes which have caught their interest. All try to give their work a shape, but the form in which each piece is finally presented varies considerably from group to group. Some show a series of loosely linked scenes, using a narrator to give them coherence; others show the influence of television as the action cuts swiftly from one location to another. Here, it is interesting to see the use of a device which Shakespeare found useful from time to time: a new location is specifically referred to in the first lines of a scene and is thus quickly and efficiently established. A few groups observe the unities and skilfully compress the action to produce what is in effect a short one-act play.

The treatments, too, vary. One group approaches the theme facetiously and their Youth in Revolt overpower their elders by remorselessly plying them with a series of dreadful jokes until they surrender and concede their demands. Another group sets a serious and thoughtful scene in Victorian times. Although their treatment is a worthier one than the other groups' it is less successful because their portrait of life in another era is not sufficiently evocative or human. However, more research will overcome this deficiency and the group will probably wish to work on this idea for a while, refining it, making it more authentic, smoothing out the weak points in the development – they are a serious, academically inclined collection and their interest has been caught by the difference between the 1880's and our own time. They decide to spend some of their time in the library before doing any more in the play itself.

Towards the end of the period, some groups are ready to show what they have prepared to the rest of the class, so we stop the general work. The groups who are not ready will have opportunities in future weeks, for we shall be exploring this theme in a number of ways and quite a bit of lesson time will be given to group work on the idea, though this will be varied with work for individuals and for the whole class. The children themselves organise the seating of the audience – each group is quite likely to want a different arrangement, though some have no preference. They automatically work 'arena' and their performances are not projected in any particular direction. Afterwards, comments are asked for, given freely and accepted without offence. Some of the points are minor technical ones, referring perhaps to an inadequate piece of mime or a slip in speech, but showing that the whole piece of work has been followed attentively; other points deal with wider matters such as the shape or development of the scene or the depth of characterisation. The comments are not exclusively critical; particular points are singled out for commendation – a neat piece of business, a well-sustained characterisation, an arresting piece of plotting. If the group feels that a comment is unjust, the members will argue back, but if it is just and reasonably expressed they take note, accept the point, and sometimes try out a suggestion there and then. Some groups who were ready are not going to be able to share their work with the others because there is not enough time. Most of them will keep the ideas in mind, discussing or working on them during the week and then, after some more practice next week, will perform them. But if the life has gone out of the idea by then they will not attempt to revive it just for the sake of performance.

It is a pity to try to force each group to work in exactly the same way – one week scripts, the next purely improvisation, and so on. They learn from the way they approach an idea and the value is in the work done, and in the measurement of achievement against intention. It is important, too, that each group should achieve a variety of approaches. For some of them, it is very easy to arrive at a slick, undemanding formula – often based on second-hand ideas, perhaps a slightly amended re-presentation of an already third-rate television script – and to reproduce this sort of thing week after week without real involvement, without real thought or effort, without extension. The superficial reproduction of indifferent material cannot really be of benefit to anyone – always accepting the fact that, when one is starting work under very difficult conditions, getting something is better, generally, than getting nothing at all. Without individual considera- tion and advice a group can tend to fall into the same pattern, to go on and on producing minor variants of the same basic approach. The group which always produces a script should be encouraged on occasions to try to be less cautious and use a less carefully structured approach from time to time. Similarly the lot who quickly – and often superficially – produce a slick but unconsidered scene each time should experience the discipline of an agreed script, at least some of which can be written down without undue hardship. A script is not necessarily more valuable than a free improvisation; it has a different function, and all the groups should have as wide an experience as possible of the different ways of going about the making of original Drama.

I allowed this class to choose their own groups; indeed, I usually did, though I know that some people hold strongly that they should not. I think that one needs considerable knowledge of the children to make valid groupings for them, and if groupings are to be imposed then they should be considered and balanced very carefully indeed. It is no good, for instance, dumping a painfully shy child into the middle of a confident, extrovert group and expecting her to be transformed. Similarly, just putting people together at random is hardly the way to produce a viable, productive – or happy – group. Allowing all the bouncy, naughty boys to gravitate to one corner and all the stolid, unresponsive girls to settle in another is not really desirable either. Here again, it is better not to let any one pattern become fixed and sacrosanct.

When children begin to feel: 'But we *always* do it this way', a change of approach is overdue. Once any pattern has become automatic and undemanding, the work is in danger of becoming sterile. Sooner or later, some children will want to work with 'proper' scripts and it is as well to have a good variety of these available. Over-compartmentalising can be unnecessarily restricting; it can be very interesting and useful for a group which has produced an original improvisation to be able to compare it with a script which has similarities of theme or treatment.

Some people do not approve of the discussion of work, and obviously there is a danger that destructive or ill-natured criticism can be damaging for children, especially the less confident. But this should not arise in a controlled situation. If it is likely to, then it could be avoided, but it would be a pity if the classroom atmosphere did not prove conducive to sensible evaluation, presented and received without acrimony.

Damaging or negative comment should be avoided, but if the emphasis is placed right from the beginning on constructive comment, on discussion directed where necessary by the teacher, there is no need for children to be hurt by what is said. Children welcome consideration of their work; to be worthy of this can enhance its value to them. But, again, no procedure is immutable and sometimes it is surely appropriate to share the work, enjoy it, and leave it at that.

This class had been working on one aspect of a wider theme, and in fact their full consideration of this topic, Revolution, occupied most of the term in one form or another. In the early stages of their work, though, I had not attempted to develop one overall idea but had moved from one approach to another as I felt they were ready for a change. Often a lesson would be given over to improvisations on one individual topic, like 'Escape' or 'Retaliation'. Sometimes, I would give them the beginning of a story and ask them to finish it for me in their own way. On other occasions, I gave them a last line: 'I have come back!'; 'Look out, it's falling!'; 'What shall we do? It's gone!' Once one starts on this idea, the lines suggest themselves readily and they would build a scene which finished with that line, often combined with a tableau position. I found this useful for classes which went on and on and never seemed to be able to bring themselves to finish a piece of improvisation. The initial stimulus could come from a picture, from press cuttings or headlines, from sounds on tape, half a dozen random objects given to a group to work into a scene, from masks, hats, or a few bits of costume. At other times, one could stimulate them with an imaginative or fantastic situation: 'Show, in your play, how you came to be driving some most unusual vehicle in a most unusual place, at its maximum speed', or the perennial: 'You take something which has a most unusual effect, and you . . .', or a title would be sufficient: 'The accident at the waxworks' (What is the fascination which waxworks hold for children? They relish plays on the subject.); or 'We only wanted to help'.

c

With some groups one could have great fun (and so could they) with a version of a parlour game. For instance: one person from each group collects a piece of paper from each of three piles and thus receives a random name of someone who is supposed to say what is quoted on a second piece of paper, in the place named on the third. Great ingenuity is needed to create plausibility in a scene in which the Prime Minister says, 'Excuse me, but your wooden leg's fallen off' at the bottom of the sea. There are lots of Drama-based games like this, and I have used them unashamedly to liven up a dull class or situation, to fill an odd gap at the end of a particular piece of work, or to bring a term to a genial conclusion. Other subjects often provide ideas which prove fruitful in Drama work.

The important thing is to have ample material readily available to provide each class or group with whatever it needs to extend its range: one collection produces neat plots but needs work on the development of character; another has a feeling for dramatic moments but lacks the facility to unify its work and present it as a satisfying whole; another is strong on humour but lacks sensitivity; yet another organises its work meticulously but communicates no pleasure or excitement. I worry somewhat when I see a document headed, say, 'First Year Drama. Scheme of work', followed by a series of headings which are to be put into operation universally, inflexibly, in immutable sequence.

III

Thursday morning before lunch. Fourth year boys this time, the male complement of three classes, brought together while the girls are working on subjects of feminine interest. The room is very full indeed, for there always seem to be far more boys in the 'lower' streams, and these three classes are supposedly the least able academically in their year, though you would not gain that impression from this lesson, which is in addition to their normal complement of S & D time and has come about through a timetable eccentricity. At the moment, the period is devoted to talks, given individually or in pairs, on subjects of their own choice. At first, the idea had been met with minimal enthusiasm – a number of them didn't relish the idea of preparing and delivering the talks themselves; even more, they felt that the others' talks were likely to prove extremely boring. With these boys, anything which involves them in activity is far more welcome than something which means that they have to sit down and listen. Indeed, this is the reason for the low placing of a number of them, for they have misapplied their energy in some more academic subjects, or have not been encouraged to apply it properly, and so have not made the progress they could have made.

I felt that this was something they should try, and in any case there was not room for activity in this, the only classroom available at that time. I had planned other work to follow this, almost as a reward, and initially I had planned to include four or five talks, followed by questions, in each forty-five minute period, to ensure variety, and because I felt it unlikely that anyone would be able to sustain interest for any length of time. As a further incentive, I had initiated a competition with a book token as prize for the best talk. However, all that soon changed and I was forced to revise my initial premises – and so were they.

I had called for volunteers for the first talk and so had those who were probably the most enthusiastic to start it off. As it was, this first talk had set the pattern for the rest. It had occupied the entire period and we had in fact to curtail the questioning at lunch time, though informal discussion went on long after the talk had finished. The idea of working in four or five talks a lesson now seemed quite impracticable, and from that first lesson onwards we now had one speaker and one reserve each week. The idea of the competition, too, had to be put aside, for we all agreed that any choice would be invidious, though I would not necessarily avoid a competition at another time if it seemed to provide a useful stimulus. Before they began the talks I gave some preliminary advice on, among other

27

points, the most effective use of notes and illustrative material, on the use of the blackboard and prepared diagrams (an overhead projector would have been most useful, but we didn't have one then). I insisted, too, that answering questions fully and lucidly was an important part of the talk. The first talk was on fishing, which proved to be a very popular subject, for we had a number more on this subject, all very informative and interesting – and today we are to have another. This information is not greeted with 'Fishing *again!*' in indignant tones, but with equivalent words uttered with enthusiasm.

It is possible to consider this question of talking rather too readily as something separate and possibly even rather special. I once heard a child coming from an English lesson calling excitedly, 'Hey! We're doing *Talks!*' The enthusiasm was gratifying, but not the implications of this particular singling out. After all, a child – or an adult for that matter – communicates information, experience, views far more usually by the spoken word than by the written. Even children we normally think of as inarticulate can readily establish fluent oral communication with their peers, outside the classroom. Often, it is only the conditions that prove inhibiting to the child. If the classroom is still looked on as the place where 'one does not speak or else', then it is hardly surprising if any child, called upon to talk, finds it impossible to overcome his conditioned feeling that this is not a proper activity in a place where he has far more often been commanded to stop talking than to start.

Especially for the child who cannot read or write fluently, speech is the essential mode of communication, and it is very wrong to assume that, because a child cannot write down information or opinion, he has nothing to express – and equally wrong to consider what he has to express as less worthy of consideration because it is not presented in one particular form. On one occasion, a Nuffield word count exercise was being undertaken with three boys, one with a very high IQ, one average, and one 'remedial'. A reporter from a national newspaper came to write about it and stayed some time with them while they talked fluently on a range of subjects. At the end, he still had no idea of the supposed academic range. Judging by the way they talked, they had seemed, to him, simply three boys talking, without a great deal to choose between them.

If children have consistently been discouraged from talking in classrooms (and I should emphasise that I know that there are occasions when conversation is certainly inappropriate) and the result is that they are disinclined to talk even when required to do so, it is even more important that they should be encouraged to put their ideas orally. Just as everyone is supposed to have enough material for one novel, so each child can manage at least one talk – indeed, after the first success, he will not wish to be limited to one. Nor is it difficult for children to engage the attention of their peers. The most difficult class I ever took used to finish their week with a double period with me, each side having already had more experience of the other than it wished for. Whatever I did, the lesson was a trial for them and for me. But if one of them took over that time and talked to the rest about animals or electrical circuits, or another showed them his puppets and explained how they worked, they were docile and interested and their questions showed their understanding. But, in those days, I always had an uneasy feeling that if I was not actively initiating the work in any particular lesson, nothing of any value would be done.

The speaker has prepared his talk well; during break, he has covered two blackboards with useful diagrams. He also has an expensive array of equipment laid out and is keeping an eye on it. I note from my place at the back that he has employed my own device of the folded envelope marked with easily legible headings and he glances quickly at this from time to time. At one point, he is explaining casting and ledgering. There is an appeal for a demonstration, but the room is crammed with humanity. He jumps quickly out of the window on to the grass outside and we crowd to the windows and applaud the display which is repeated until an upstairs window is sharply opened and there is an irascible cry from a teacher whose class is being distracted from his piece of exposition. After the talk, there are many knowledgeable comments and pertinent questions and they are answered fluently and accurately.

It would have been valuable to have taped the talks so that each person giving one could have settled down later on to his own study of what he had achieved. Not with the rest of the class around; just running a tape through to re-hear what was said can be a pointless and time-wasting activity. Imaginatively used, tape recorders can be most useful, but a lot of us do not go beyond the simple superficial uses. I certainly didn't, for a long time. I never thought of preparing tapes for use in conjunction with work in progress or of giving plenty of opportunity for individual listening to tapes, as important a part of the use of tape recorders as individual reading is of books.

One talk I remember with embarrassment – my own. They decided that I ought to give a talk, and I thought it would be valuable to give one on the technical aspects of speech. I prepared it carefully, feeling that the group would be knowledgeably critical. They proved to be most interested in all the technicalities, feeling their soft palates with delight and contorting their lips to produce pure vowel sounds. At the end, I demonstrated some instances of technically imperfect speech which were received with enthusiasm bordering on ecstasy. I was totally unaware of the reason for this until the next week, when some of them encouraged me to 'be a sport' and repeat some of my imitations of members of the staff.

IV

Tuesday afternoon. A mixed collection of third year pupils, boys and girls, of estimated average ability. One group has volunteered to work on and present a 'How Not to do It' sketch, a melodrama which I have drawn up for them, giving opportunity for a wide range of technical errors and inadequacies. Their stage is cluttered with furniture, their entrances are badly placed, their timing and pace is consistently at fault, their properties are missing, or don't function as they should. They have put a lot of work into it and the result is very amusing. After that, the audience is encouraged to pull the thing apart. The group sustain the joke by defending their production as ineptly as they staged it. Everyone enjoys the exercise and learns from it – probably far more than from a straightforward technical exposition, for they have to identify the fault, analyse it, then consider how it could be put right. Just for interest, the group agree to try it again, seriously, stipulating only that the line: 'You fool! You have shot your own father!' which ends the sketch must be cut, for they feel that it could not be delivered seriously to a six-footer about a diminutive prone body. Although the lines are deliberately melodramatic and the plot is not strong, a surprising difference is made by following the critical suggestions.

Most of the groups are working on their contributions for an informal school festival which is to be held in a few weeks' time, and they have become interested in the technicalities of stage craft. Some of them already have some of the leaflets which I had given out from time to time, giving some information on this; some regularly and critically go to plays, particularly the fairly frequent school and PTA productions; some are just becoming interested in the idea of putting on a production and now feel a need for greater technical background. They have enjoyed their Drama work up to now, but being essentially organisers rather than performers they are beginning to be attracted to the idea of actually mounting their own plays rather than being involved in other people's. Probably a straight talk on techniques would not have been equally useful for all these categories, but this lighthearted approach has amused them even when it did not engage their critical faculties. (Which it did, most of the time.)

Next, the hall curtains are drawn and everyone goes on to

31

the stage for a demonstration on the use of the switchboard and lighting. In the festival, each group is entirely responsible for all its own backstage work, including the lighting. Although that generally means that, under supervision, a fairly small group of boys – and a couple of girls – finish up doing most of the work, nevertheless the children in groups, and especially the producers, need to know what they are asking for and how it can be achieved – if it can be achieved.

'When I say, 'Yare, yare, good Iras,' I want the very beginnings of the sunset in the sky,' says one producing Cleopatra. 'Can I have that?'

'You can have anything you like – you're doing it. The sort of things you want, you won't get anyone else to.'

This cavalier response is Cleopatra'd over and the demonstrator agrees to take over the lighting for her extracts from Act V in addition to the others he has undertaken. They remain on the stage, discussing lighting, occasionally leaping to the floor to examine an effect.

'It's not enough.'

'How can you tell? It's not striking anything – except the floor. Look, stand in it. How's that?'

'It's not enough. At least, it's not *luminous* enough.'

The gap between artistic intention and practicability is slowly narrowed and eventually a resolution will be reached. When they have finished, others will move on to the switchboard. Until then, they work in various parts of the hall, after an argument about whether the House lights should be on or not. The activity is varied. One group of about a dozen is working on the choral speaking of a poem written by one of their number, not a sensitive poem, but brash, rhythmic, onomatopoeic. It was specially written as an experiment to try to produce a poem which, like Vachel Lindsay's 'The Congo', would make its effect most readily by being spoken aloud. The group is not at present working harmoniously, for there is a difference of opinion between those who, though willing to create effects by lengthening vowel sounds or strongly emphasising consonants, are unwilling to allow extraneous noises like humming, whistling, or clicking of fingers. The other side is not only prepared to use these devices but also to experiment with combinations of speech and movement. Although the argument is lengthy and could perhaps be considered to waste time, it is essentially one which they must resolve for themselves, after full consideration. Eventually, they agree that the writer should make the decision, which she does, in favour of the experimental approach – after all, she says, she wrote the poem as an experiment in sound. Agreement is general but one point is raised: if the poem is intended as such as experiment, would it not be sensible to allow at least some of it to make its own sound, without additions? This point is conceded and the work continues.

Other groups are polishing the life out of their improvisations. When this becomes tedious they turn more profitably to considering the technicalities involved in presenting them. One scene is set in a crowded discothèque which requires a thick, smoky atmosphere and they discuss how to produce this. (We used a 'guaranteed non-noxious' tablet which, when burned, filled stage and hall with choking smoke and emptied them of people. After that, we used dry ice, though we had some noteworthy failures with that, too.) Others are tackling one-act plays or excerpts from longer plays. Some have selected scenes from Shakespeare. A large portion of the last act of *Hamlet* is having difficulty with some plastic rapiers which look most realistic but snap immediately on being put to any hard use. They will have to make some new ones of cane or wood and this will mean in turn making considerable amendments to the long, painstakingly worked-out duel. While the protagonists are discussing this, the rest decide on their costumes.

Another group, working on Act III, Scene III, from *Macbeth*, have an unorthodox approach to the question of presentation. They are to dress in motor-cycling gear and even plan to have a motor cycle on the stage, revving up. Their approach leads to minor textual amendments. They consider changing 'His horses go about' to refer to a more modern form of transport, but this does not prove feasible – each substitution leads to giggles, so they leave the line out. Then they find that this makes a difference to the next speech, so they have to reconsider. In fact, the text is not the prime consideration in this treatment which is extremely athletic and has involved much prior work in the gym. These lively, clever, but not academically inclined boys do not generally achieve their full potential. Their improvisation work has always been good, lively and alert, but at first they shied away from the very name Shakespeare. However, they were encouraged to tackle this scene partly because it was extremely short, partly because of the opportunity it offered for a well-mounted fight and partly because I had told them that they could choose exactly how they wanted to tackle it. This has reassured them that, though deferring to the establishment in their choice of an author, their individuality has nevertheless been preserved by their iconoclastic approach to him. Of course, the idea of modern-dress Shakespeare is not original, but it is original to them, and so is the creative process which has brought the scene into being in this way. They have learned the lines almost without thinking about it and their speaking of them is intelligent and vital.

One or two children are preparing poems, extracts from books and speeches from plays for the speech section of the festival. This event will last a week and include categories for movement work, individual and group speaking, improvisation, original plays, extracts from Shakespeare and from other plays. Unlike a number of classes, this one is not planning a corporate entry, one piece of work involving them all, but they could have done if they had so chosen. The festival is completely non-competitive. If it were, it is quite possible that Cleopatra could be placed last. But as it is, she will have the chance to play the part to an audience which, because it will include her family and friends, will be at least predominately sympathetic and at least in part congratulatory. It is unlikely that she will again have the chance to play the part and she is enjoying herself. And, of course, she is involved in an experience which is very important to her.

As children develop, they need the opportunity to try out different approaches for themselves. Initially, choice may well need directing and one must always encourage individuals or groups not to settle in the pattern but to try new ideas or approaches. Some people argue strongly against allowing them to tackle sections from plays, and especially Shakespeare's plays. One such argument held that if they selected bits they enjoyed they would later lack the relish necessary to encourage them to swallow the unpalatable remainder. While I see the point of this argument, my own experience leads me to think otherwise. The *Macbeth* group, for instance, later took the same parts – the whole of them – in a full, traditionally-costumed production of the play. If they had not first done the excerpt, I could not possibly have persuaded them to tackle parts in Shakespeare. As it was, this experience convinced them that he wrote plays which were exciting to act. They brought their own understanding to Act III, Scene I, which, far from being the somewhat tedious stretch which it can be sometimes in amateur performances, acutely conveyed the mood of rejection and disillusion. Avoidance of mystique enabled the children to approach these plays with enthusiasm as primarily material for performance. I am not of course saying that they should not be studied, but I certainly hold that they should not *only* be studied – it is quite wrong that children should go through their school lives – and even now some do – regarding Shakespeare only as printed words, to be discussed, analysed, studied, but never performed.

Festivals provide a very useful stimulus, if they are the right sort of festival. I see no reason why a festival for children of this age (indeed, I would hold that this applies for any age or stage) should be competitive. Competition which tells some groups that they are the losers is a negation of the very title of festival, which should be enjoyable – festive, in fact. When I used to adjudicate youth drama festivals, however hard I tried to encourage the beginners or the less experienced groups, if I then had to announce that they had come last – or, worse still, recite the marks awarded – a lot of groups were so discouraged that they gave up Drama. On the other hand, I do not hold that any public gathering together of children's work must necessarily be a negation of all we are trying to do. Provided that they have acquired some basis for evaluating their own work and measuring their own view of it against that of other people, it is surely rather sterile for their work to have to blush consistently unseen. For these children, at this stage of their development, it was right that they should discipline and concentrate their efforts in working towards public presentation. They were not toddlers being involved in work which they did not understand, producing a nostalgic response from their audiences; nor would any precocity be allowed to pass unnoticed or undealt with by their contemporaries. The individual verse speakers were most prone to narcissism, but their category was included as an act of public relations to mollify those people who found improvisation work disquieting if couched in local dialect and vernacular, however appropriate this might be to the situation. At that time, regional accents were not quite the thing; nowadays, they are far more acceptable.

V

Wednesday afternoon. Although I am scheduled to take this group, I am also due to spend some of the afternoon with other groups. However, they no longer need more than occasional advice, and my comments are now presented and received as personal, rather than official, pronouncements. There are about thirty sixth-formers in this collection, though they are not all in the hall where the lesson is based. One group of about a dozen are falling about with laughter on the field where their endless (literally; it was never finished, though it ran to hundreds of feet) film about a boy's fantasies in a boring lesson is being made. A number of Indians, equipped with head-dresses and bows and arrows but riding bicycles, are attempting a sequence in which some of them become involved with the Rugby posts. The unsuccessful attempts are far more numerous – and funnier – than the successful ones. In a small room close to the hall, four or five boys are working with a tape recorder. One of them has brought along a mixer and other equipment of his own. The piece of work they are getting on to the tape is not particularly original but it is technically expert. Some of them have a strong interest in electronics and are very concerned that the tape should reproduce well when they play it to a gathering of fellow sixth-formers on the same occasion as another of the groups presents the first act of *Skin of Our Teeth*. Their progress is slow, but meticulous. I suggest that they might try a tape/slide link-up, but they are not keen. Their overwhelming interest at the moment is with producing an aural effect, not a visual one. As it happens, their specialist subjects are scientific, but this does not mean that the scientists are only concerned with the technicalities. There are scientists in each of the other collections. One is playing Mr Antrobus in *Skin Of Our Teeth*, and is doing very well. In fact, the whole rehearsal of that act is going well, rather surprisingly, for I had not expected such a mixed collection of dominant personalities could possibly manage a successful production in the way which they had chosen to do it. They agreed to try a group production, developed by discussion and with no official producer in charge. They had originally intended to do a reading production, but today they begin to find the books a nuisance and they decide that, as they already know a lot of it from the work they have done so far, they will learn the rest. A dinosaur wanders round, wrapped in the remains of a fur coat, memorising 'It's cold'.

Two pairs of boys work, just for the pleasure of it, on the opening duologue of *Waiting for Godot*. It is most interesting to note the difference in their approach. When they are ready, each pair will perform for the other and for anyone else who is interested to see, compare and discuss the two interpretations. Another pair, boy and girl this time, work on the second act from *Private Lives* and find it quite a change from *Miss Julie*.

Drama is still for everyone, not just for the specialists. Sometimes, the odd idea is propounded that, when they reach the sixth form, the scientists, the linguists, the mathematicians – the artists, even – should now start the serious business of specialising and ignore fringe subjects such as Drama. They have, the argument goes, really nothing to gain from them now that specialisation is upon them. I disagree.

The pattern continues to develop. The initial enthusiasm and intuitive involvement of the first year children has been developed, supported by technical knowledge, by self-knowledge, by experience. The development is not complete – it never is – and complacency will slow it, or stop it altogether.

If things have gone as they should, the role of the Drama teacher has now changed radically. He is no longer the prime mover and sole inspiration. He still has to encourage, to advise, to create opportunities, to ensure that right attitudes continue to develop. But he has undoubtedly moved from the UC position to another, well DR, which is not all that easy for some of us. Certainly not for me, but it does lead nevertheless to a completely different kind of satisfaction.

Chapter 2

Production

Every school year we did one main production for each of the first, second, third and fourth years. After that, we felt that they should do their own (see section on 'Impetus'). This was because we were a very large school and one production a year would not have given an opportunity for a large proportion of the children to take part. It helped, incidentally, to overcome the idea that a play was a rather mystic and special ritual, generally for initiates, only to be indulged in once a year, and then under carefully structured circumstances. This pattern of productions suited a large comprehensive school. Previously I had been well satisfied with far less.

At my first school I had only mounted one production in six years, really because I simply hadn't thought about doing one before that. But when we devised our own version of *Everyman* in English lessons, we gathered two more plays to go with it and make an evening's entertainment. I felt this was rather a daring innovation, and I think we all enjoyed the disruption and the spurious sense of importance which being concerned in The Play gave us.

In my next school, one production a year was as much as I could manage, and the first of them, *Androcles and the Lion*, sharply diminished my enthusiasm. I found it difficult to get the children to come to rehearsals – and indeed, one performer, who thoroughly enjoyed the first performance, went carol singing on the second night, and someone had to read his part in. It was very hard work, but later I was glad that I had not given up, as I was tempted to at the time. Each year I used the same, very talented boy (who later became a successful professional actor) to play the lead and I built up a small production team who were involved in the work of each successive production.

Colleagues and friends were wonderfully helpful over costumes and settings, but everyone who helped carried far too great a burden. All the children in the team gained considerable pleasure from what they did; standards improved and we became more ambitious. Our final production was a creditable *Macbeth* which I remember, among other things, for the genuine, uninhibited cheer which greeted the appearance of the defeated tyrant's head, so impressively modelled that the less sophisticated members of the audience believed that we had dared the ultimate in realism – without stopping to consider that it was only the first night. Also worthy of applause were the performances of at least two of the cast who could read only with considerable difficulty yet had not only learned their lines perfectly but spoke them with meaning and sensitivity. Nevertheless, I was only working with an enthusiastic coterie and the productions were unrelated to the life of the rest of the school. Staff and parents supported well; the Dress Rehearsal for the school aroused great enthusiasm. Even so, the feeling that I had fostered was that these were enjoyable but specialist things only to be done by the select few.

Therefore when I came to a large, new school, with no established patterns and with considerable opportunity for experiment, I determined to try to establish a wider basis for productions. In the first and second years, I aimed to include all those who wanted to be included so as to give a chance to everyone who wished to take part in at least a couple of main productions during their school life. One year could contain up to four hundred children, so if too many people wanted to take part, then it was first come first served – in one production of *The Boy With a Cart* we stopped at two hundred, which really was too many. Later we found that a hundred and fifty was the absolute maximum, but this required a play with plenty of scope for crowd and movement.

In the third and fourth years, although I generally worked with fairly large numbers they were nowhere near the gargantuan proportions of the junior productions. I had other limitations in this age range: at that time it was not considered advisable to use children who were in their O-level year. Though I didn't really agree with this, it was school policy. Another pattern emerged for these age groups, then. In the third year I gave opportunities to those who would be barred in their next year because they were engaged in less frivolous matters; in the fourth year, I used those who were not taking their exams till the next year. I tried the idea of parallel productions, doing the same play – *A Midsummer Night's Dream* one year, *Macbeth* the next – both productions on the same week, playing on alternate nights. It made a fascinating comparison, watching a younger, more academic, cast giving their interpretation of the play and then, the next night, a completely different approach by children a year older. We used the same basic setting for both productions and achieved considerable saving by redistributing the same hired costumes from one group of performers to another.

If older pupils wanted productions for themselves, they initiated them in various ways. They could produce them themselves through the Youth Wing, which children were able to join when they reached the age of fifteen. (A Youth Tutor was appointed, responsible for developing a wide range of out-of-school activities, including those which are normally associated with youth clubs.) It meant that they were responsible for all aspects of their own production – costume, setting, business management, publicity and so on. They could also get someone to produce plays for them (again, through the Youth Wing: we generally had two groups functioning at a time, though there could be as many as half a dozen plays in various stages of rehearsal at one time); or they could become involved in a joint staff–student project – emphatically not a question of the staff doing a play and letting some privileged pupils hold spears. These productions were prepared in the orthodox way, generally, with rehearsals, in evenings or holidays, over a period of time.

I must here raise a point on which I know a number of people strongly disagree with me. School productions often take far too long to put on. Sometimes, a term – or even longer – is given to rehearsals: two, three or four times a week. One scene will be taken through many times, one speech worked on over and over again until the phrasing and intonation are just as the producer wants it. I think that four weeks are ample for putting on a production – three are sufficient – if one of the weeks is given over to intensive work.

What are the arguments in favour of a longer period? To give children time to learn the parts? I wonder. We give children too little credit for their facility in learning: they learn tremendously quickly, especially in the 11–14 range. We proved this repeatedly, doing difficult plays, or long plays, or plays where the text must be given with scrupulous respect and understanding. In a semi-improvised play anyone who forgets his lines can easily improvise something else; but that would be indefensible in, say, a Shakespeare (though I have heard it done professionally). I can remember as a schoolboy successfully mastering the Shakespeare speech set for the week, even in one of my own meagre and grudging homeworks. One develops the facility as it is required. In my own amateur performances, I find that I now follow the standard amateur rules: (a) However long you have to learn your part, you generally wait till the last moment; (b) If the producer insists, you really learn; if he doesn't, you really intend to learn, sometime.

Children are tremendously keen to learn their lines, especially if being in the play is something exciting and enjoyable, not just a chore undertaken because no-one else will play Macduff. And again, the really heavy learning generally falls on only two or three people – really only on one in *Peer Gynt*, and in one of our versions of this play we used only a four-week rehearsal period. Peer, by no means a studious boy, and with no previous acting experience, managed the part with panache and verve and without strain. If a lengthy period were needed for learning, it would generally only be needed by a small proportion of the cast, and it takes considerable dedication to feed 'The Queen, my

lord, is dead' to someone over a period of ten or twelve weeks
in the belief that both you and your fellow performer are
using the time with equal profit. Once, I gave a boy a full
script of his part, which was quite lengthy. Two days later, he
came to me and told me he had lost the script. Our children
were always losing their scripts and I was magisterial – even
more so when he asked, did it matter? I told him. 'But I know
it,' he said. And he did.

Well, then, to perfect the moves and gestures? But is that
really what one wants in Drama as part of education? Even
if the producer were a great man of the theatre it would be
hard to defend such an approach in this context; and the
producer is far more likely to be simply someone with an
enthusiasm for Drama (the best sort of school producer), or
perhaps even someone who has been landed with the job
because no-one else will take it on. It needs a certain amount
of confidence to accept that the child will manage to come on,
to go off, to respond to others, to use gesture without re-
straint but with good effect, all without being coached or
bludgeoned into it. But he can. And if he couldn't, I would
still find it hard to justify the other approach.

To discuss the play and to involve the group in consideration and evaluation of the work they are interpreting is
admirable, and the value of this is readily conceded. But I
wonder how widespread this approach is in the long rehearsal
periods. I feel, too, that this approach is often more useful
with the older children, particularly the sixth form – and it
should really lead to group discussion, not simply the
producer's views expounded at length.

The danger of a lengthy rehearsal time is that the work may
well become mechanical, stale, lacking excitement or involvement. I once attended a performance of a school play which
had been rehearsed for nearly a year. It was beautifully
mounted, well spoken, impeccably grouped. At one point,
however, the smooth running was momentarily lost and,
almost as if there had been a click in the machinery, quite a
large part, a dramatic and important part, of one scene

started to be repeated. The same meticulously developed intonations, the same painstakingly timed gestures, the same impeccable graduations of pace moved inexorably before us like a re-run of some film demonstrating a technical process. Smooth, mechanical, infinitely rehearsed, but mindless, uninvolved. When the same section started for a third time, the prompter cried 'No!', voicing the general feeling.

Many more producers are now experimenting, taking risks, altering rehearsal patterns. Some still feel apprehensive about changing the approach, often because far too much prestige is involved in The School Play and they are unwilling to try anything different for fear of a discouraging failure. And the ultimate irony of that is that the traditional school productions can often still be judged by the wrong criteria. Audiences are of course necessary for full performances; they must be treated with courtesy – which means, among other things, that they should be able to see, hear and understand what is going on – but, in a school production, they are not the only, or indeed the prime, consideration.

After the fourth year, of course, it was up to the children themselves to decide how they wanted to go about their productions, one requirement being that there must be no interference at all in their school work. Some worked intensively over a holiday period, some worked in the evenings, some discussed and improvised for quite a long time before they started work on the play itself. In years one to four, though, the standard pattern was a three- to four-week rehearsal period. I must make it clear that the last week was always one of really intensive work. Anybody in the cast could be used in rehearsal when required, and they were all excused homework where necessary during that week, on the firm understanding that they contracted to make up all missed work as soon as the production was over.

At first, some teachers were inclined to feel that this arrangement caused disruption, but in fact most very soon accepted that the putting on of a school play, even conventionally, always

causes upheaval and distraction: they remembered the Week of
The Play from their own school days. Furthermore they knew
well in advance exactly when their work would be disturbed
and so they were able to plan for it and not, for example,
start a major piece of exposition during the four or five disturbed days. The contract with the children was clear, too, and
no work could be missed. A number of teachers welcomed the
opportunity to do some work of an experimental nature with
their group. It would have been even easier had there been a
less closely structured timetable.

The four rehearsal weeks needed prior thought. The idea was
to start with a small number of children, those who had most to
do or say in the play. If a beginning could be managed in holiday
time, so much the better; so our main productions often followed
a break, generally being performed early in the Spring or
Summer terms. They couldn't all be done then, though, so
sometimes the first week's rehearsals would take place in the
lunch hour or after school – rarely in the evenings with the
younger children.

Generally we had two members of staff working on the actual
production, but a number of others helped too. Some, for
instance, though having no particular knowledge of Drama,
would nevertheless arrange for children in their tutor groups to
run through some of their parts for the rest of the group who
would comment and advise, generally helpfully. Others would
spend time with children in their groups, or classes, discussing
their parts, hearing them, advising. It was help of this sort
which enabled us to use children of limited academic or
reading ability in major parts, even in Shakespeare productions.
Some staff members would wander into rehearsal sessions in their
free time and attach themselves to one group or another,
sometimes encouraging simply by being there. Some of the
pupils, too, acted as associate producers, especially during
holiday periods, taking over one scene or section; but the amount
of influence they were allowed to have depended very much on
the group itself. In the two parallel productions of *A Midsummer Night's Dream* for instance, one boy took charge of all

the third year comics' scenes, another took over the fourth year's. The first one mapped out groupings, worked on pace and timing rather as a conventional producer would, but the other was simply allowed to hold the book and to prompt only when a scene had completely come to a halt.

This help generally did not start until the second or third weeks; in the first week, we worked with the small group of children with the larger parts. That way, a considerable amount of the play could usually be covered before the others were brought into rehearsals. But with the smaller group it was possible to discuss points, to spend time on scenes without feeling guilty about the fretting character sitting in the corner missing his soccer practice as he waited for his two lines to come up. Besides, after that week, Macbeth and Lady Macbeth could rehearse when they wanted to, on their own, or just with a friend to prompt. In one intensive weekend spent this way, they could really begin to come to terms with the characters and the situations. I used to believe that no rehearsal could possibly be productive without my active involvement, but I learned otherwise.

Of course, there was no reason why the others should not have their scripts and be studying them – that is, if it was a published play. If it was one that I was writing or drawing together, bits of it tended not to be written till rather late, or not to be written at all. When the other, longer, speaking parts were brought into rehearsal pattern, then the assistant producers became very useful. Sometimes these were senior pupils, often taller than the members of staff and occasionally more authoritarian; sometimes they were contemporaries of the players; sometimes they were anyone who happened to be at hand. There was a wide range of opportunities for producers – from the one who wished to direct a fight or a movement sequence to the girl who took on the task of seeing that Peer Gynt knew his lines and who subsequently wrote for the magazine:

'The play *Peer Gynt* was an extremely long one, and the leading actor was on the stage the whole time. My job in this play was to help him to learn his lines.

We started about two and a half weeks before the performance was due to take place. We first read through the play, scene by scene, with myself reading all the other parts and Ron reading his own. After doing this two or three times, I took the script away from him and he tried to speak the lines from memory. We progressed quite quickly. One of the main drawbacks was that Ron did not seem able to hang on to his script. He kept losing it and we spent a lot of valuable time trying to borrow other people's. But apart from this things went quite smoothly . . .'

The account has its moments of over-statement (and, indeed, of understatement: the fury of a child who 'put my script down just a moment ago and someone's walked off with it' could be impressive) but its matter-of-factness gives an indication of how both the writer and the learner accepted this procedure as unremarkable.

For those who wished to try out a conventional approach, blocking in moves and so on, I had prepared a series of leaflets which gave them quite a lot of basic information and they soon became proficient at bandying 'ULC' (Upstage Left Centre) around (though this did not always rouse the awed respect they felt it should).

By this time, the setting would be under way. With this approach, it was not possible to produce an elaborate setting nor, with work on some areas of the production yet to be initiated, one which might inhibit the free development of those scenes. We found that a general pattern developed.

A variety of levels was essential, especially with large-cast plays, and we also needed easy flow on and off the stage area. In doing crowd scenes, I found that the various levels almost automatically led to pleasing groupings and so too did the fact that the grouping did not have to cease sharply at the front of the platform, for we had a large, clumsy, noisy but infinitely useful sets of steps which led by broad, shallow treads from floor to stage level. We tended not to have naturalistic settings – though obviously senior productions of *Private Lives* or *The Caretaker* called for box sets – picaresque plays where the action flowed swiftly from one place to another would have to be slowed intolerably by continual set changes.

Cheapness was another quality which commended itself, and we found imaginative use of material which, though unusual, was readily available often produced visually exciting results. For a production of the Chester Cycle, we balanced one gothic archway with a fresco of scaffolding borrowed from the builders who were then completing the school building. In *A Midsummer Night's Dream*, playing the court scenes on a forestage backed by the red velvet curtains allowed us to use the inner stage, draped in swathes of black agricultural polythene, as a most atmospheric forest, which, however, got us into a lot of trouble with the Fire Officer. One production of *Peer Gynt* was played in a setting of thick strands of rope. *The Boy With a Cart* was the first of a number of productions in which we used back projections of easily changeable slides made by sticking Cinamoid on glass which had been cut to size. For this, we hired a special lantern with a wide-angle lens from Strand Electric and a large back-projection screen from Projection and Display Services Ltd, but we later found that we could use a variety of approaches. For some productions, we back-projected 35 mm slides and later we made our own 35 mm colour slides using only Cinamoid, with no glass. We tried front projection, too, but this only worked when heads and bodies didn't get in the way (though you can get interesting results by experimenting with projecting colour slides on to the groups of moving people, particularly if they are dressed in pale colours). In a mock Victorian production, we used the device of the stage within a stage, making it from Dexion, an invaluable aid to quick and simple setting. The rest of the acting area, which represented our own environment, was featureless, but the little 'stage' showed local settings thinly disguised as pantomime settings and kept to manageable proportions.

When we did arena productions – about one in three of our output – we often found that no setting at all was needed. *Transformation Scene* was presented with only a rostrum, a screen and flimsy hangings. A more elaborate setting might well have been distracting and the imaginative quality of the children evoked the settings more effectively than any scenery we could have produced: after all, however realistic scenery is, the audience knows that it *is* scenery. For this production, I made use also of two other great aids to setting: lighting, and the performers themselves. When the scene changed from the darkening evening following the performance to the land of perpetual happiness, all that happened was that the area was filled with warm, bright light and with children dressed in bright colours carrying garlands, flowers, brilliant banners. The area was transformed.

Even when the acting area was an empty arena or a bare platform with only a variety of levels to break it up and only mobiles of polystyrene snowflakes for setting, I found that flexible use of lighting could transform these: one spotlight on a person isolates him; a change of emphasis in lighting from one area to another automatically switches the attention of the audience. And beyond the purely practical uses which lighting has in focusing the attention, it can in itself transform the whole mood and character of the setting – the *Peer Gynt* rope-bedecked set, sometimes lit from in front, sometimes from behind, from above, from below, from the side, took on a whole gamut of different moods and qualities.

Gradually the pattern of the final performance began to emerge. It was often a rather tenuous pattern when, as often happened with our first and second year pupils, the play was original. This was not chauvinism or excess of zeal but necessity. At one point it became difficult, almost impossible, to find plays which gave the sort of scope we needed for the younger children. Nowadays, with the many new Drama publications for schools it is much easier; but at that time, when we had all just put a great deal of energy and enthusiasm into a play which left us feeling very dissatisfied, there seemed to be strong arguments for writing our own.

At that point, I reconsidered an idea I had had in mind for some time, that of doing a modern version of *Pilgrim's Progress*, which turned out to be the forerunner of quite a number of our own plays. In such a project, one could see considerable scope for the use of large numbers, opportunity for movement, dance routine and crowd work. I drew up a scenario and started to write the scenes which seemed most amenable, completing about a third of the play, most of the script being of the opening parts. It then occurred to some of my colleagues that this material could be stimulating if used in various lessons as a focus for work. One Religious Education teacher initiated the idea of modern parables with her class. They produced a number of very good ones. (I will not reproduce one here because they are available in *Pilgrim '70*.) Other colleagues became interested in the idea and their classes began to supply me with dialogue for snobbish women, fiends of Hell, Giant Despair, and with inanities for Pliable and Worldly Wisemen. I used the best of the dialogue and ideas to construct appropriate scenes. Even before we started our intensive week of rehearsal, therefore, the children were conversant with the ideas of the play and felt involved in it. So, in that last week, though the play was yet to be drawn together (on the morning of the first performance as it happened) the children understood the approach and already felt that this was very much their own project.

A rehearsal on the Monday of the final week of *Pilgrim '70* probably did not look much like a rehearsal in the conventional sense. In the hall there were a lot of scripts in evidence, some being learned, some being written, extended or amended. The three children whose parables were being included had each collected a group of friends and they were working out the action which would accompany the spoken parable. It was up to them to ask for advice if they needed it, but they did not have to if they felt they were managing well enough. Their responsibility was to have the scene ready for presentation when required. Occasionally, people from other groups would drift along and offer comments or suggestions. On the stage, Pilgrim and Faithful were spending pleasantly superfluous time on working out their short contest and fight. They soon found out that scripts were inhibiting at this point and so engaged

Appolyon to 'feed in' the lines to them. After a couple of runs at
this, Appolyon was no longer needed so he settled in a corner to
learn his own lines – fortunately, in addition to being by far the
tallest boy in the second year, he had also contributed a script
for the Appolyon scene, so we used that. Then, the stage was
cleared by my co-producer to work out a dance routine for the
Vanity Fair scene. Much initial confusion of right and left feet.

The activity flowed out from the hall on to the grass outside,
softer for the falls of the boy who had been persuaded to stand
in as a substitute Pilgrim in a movement sequence in which he is
given a rough time by Giant Despair's minions. This was not
supposed to involve actual physical contact, but this ideal was as
yet imperfectly realised. Farther out on the field, a satanic
group of demons were deciding which of their lines should be
spoken individually, which by small groups, which by the full
Demonology, and were practising. After a while, dissatisfied
with the results, they borrowed a drum from the music room,
and this made a lot of difference. A group of pilgrims sat on the
grass and practised their Shaker hymn, ' 'Tis the Gift to be
Simple'. In this session and in others which followed, both in and
out of school time, most of the component parts of the play
were being worked out with, where necessary, the aid of sub-
stitutes for Pilgrim. About a hundred children were engaged in
this process, far more fully than I could have managed in
conventional rehearsals. This work continued, too, at lunch-
times, after school and in the children's homes. I moved from
group to group, sometimes resisting the temptation to interfere,
sometimes not – and in any case generally being asked for
opinion or advice. At this stage, my energy was better con-
served; we had yet to tackle the crowd scenes.

The first time we did the Vanity Fair crowd scene, the hall
was disturbingly full of children. I had said that anyone who
was not already taking part and wished to be involved could
come along to the rehearsal and we would see if we could fit
them in. I soon began to feel overwhelmed by the response to my
unconsidered invitation. However, when they were sat down,
they looked less daunting, as children generally do when their

mobility is restricted. I also made them put out their chairs in approximately audience positions, in straight lines, leaving gangways in the centre and at the sides. This further neutralised the effect of massed groups of child and was also valuable when we came to the actual rehearsal of the scene, for I had found that, with large numbers in the cast, it was advisable to rehearse as far as possible in the same physical conditions as those in which performances would take place. I once did an arena production in which appeared a large number of creatures, each with a large papier mâché, wire-framed head, with eyeholes adequate for seeing in open conditions. In rehearsals, we had just let them disperse when they came to the end of their scenes, but in performance they had to channel themselves off through a relatively narrow, dark, curtained area. The consequent panic was alarming: blind, panic-stricken children thumped heavily and sightlessly into one another, battering enormous heads against others, losing all sense of direction and lurching frantically back into the acting area, treading shredded papier mâché underfoot and shrieking hollow, indistinguishable instructions at one another.

We first ran through the skeleton of the scene for the watchers. The speakers had already fully rehearsed this. It would have been a waste of time and an open invitation for chaos if we had tried to shape and rehearse the speaking parts with the rest of the players around. As it was, the onlookers saw how the scene was shaped and understood what was going on. Then we ran it through again for them while I explained the crowd's function, stopping the action where necessary to indicate, for instance, where they came on, where parts of the acting area had to be cleared for the trial or the dancers, where they were expected to 'freeze', where the focus of their attention had to swing from one centre to another. All purely practical points, no interpretive matters – I found I could not deal satisfactorily with both at the same time, initially. As they seemed to have grasped the main points, I refrained from running the scene through again, though it would perhaps have been wiser if I had. The actual moment of initiating crowd work always finds me reluctant to

act, but we had now reached a decisive point. I indicated to
them the various places through which they could make their
entrances: the doors at the back of the hall which gave access to
the three aisles, another fairly wide doorway close to the side of
the stage, and a very narrow entrance, the only one to lead
directly from the backstage area on to the stage itself. I
reminded the cast of their cue for entering, which was visual and
easily remembered, so I did not feel it necessary to make them
all chant it to me; after Pilgrim and Faithful had discussed the
city of Vanity Fair which lay ahead of them, they left the
acting area which then slowly filled with the inhabitants. Then
we started.

The situation was complicated by the fact that I was called
away briefly to the phone shortly before the scene began and
by the time I got back my co-producer, whose first experience of
crowd work this was, was crying 'Stop! Stop!'; in a voice which
could not penetrate the hubbub, and was contemplating using
a whistle. We let the scene grind to a halt, which it eventually
did in an ungainly but good-humoured way, with crowds of
children standing round in unprepossessing clumps, giggling,
while others gradually abandoned the struggle to get on to the
acting area through the one narrow entry which the majority
had selected, and the speakers, visually and aurally swamped,
used their elbows to carve out enough space to stand on. It had
been invaluable: there is nothing to match a resounding disaster
for bringing inadequacies home to people. We all sat down again.

It was important to retain the feeling of enjoyment, though
it required some effort. A show of temperament at this stage
would have proved discouraging for the children and tiring
for me so the comment was deliberately made lightly. They
knew it had been a mess and the practical experience was far
more valuable to them than a series of abstract exhortations.
As each point was raised, they related it to what had gone
wrong, saw why it had gone wrong and how it could be improved.
I was helped in my exposition by the larkings of a light-hearted
group who took it upon themselves to illustrate my words with
actions.

Obviously, I said, they had not made proper use of all the
entrances available to them. If a crowd assembled in the local
shopping centre, they would not all have made their way
through one narrow entrance. Nor would they all have arrived
at exactly the same time or at exactly the same pace. Some
would be wandering, looking at the shops, some would be
hurrying, some coming on their own, some with families, others
with groups of friends. And they would all be real people, all
different, individual. Here, the interpretive point facilitated
the technical one – once the children had really thought and
individualised their entrances we were unlikely again to have to
face unyielding slabs of child moving in a mindless mass,
generally all to exactly the same point in the acting area. Next
I pointed out the disadvantages of groupings based on solid
masses drawn up in inexorably straight lines. My group of
demonstrators helped here, first bunching into an unyielding
block, then, perhaps somewhat over-elaborately, relaxing into a
more aesthetically pleasing positions. The rest began to see the
difference, to realise that they didn't all have to stand regimen-
tally but that they could lounge, sit, lean, sit back on their heels,
put an arm round the shoulders of a friend. Next, it was necessary to persuade them that they didn't all have to crowd on to
the platform itself but could settle on the steps – in the hall,
even, so long as they didn't block the view of the audience (my
group enjoyed demonstrating this, with some pretending to try
to watch the play while others stood, unyielding, in front of
them). We started again.

This time, the whole thing was far more natural and fluent.
The scene gradually filled with individuals and groups, all
behaving and talking as the characters they had chosen for
themselves. The groupings were not static but flexible and
interesting (the different levels helped here). The children
were enjoying themselves very much and the noise escalated.
This was the point at which one character was supposed to
introduce a group of dancers. He tried, but the crowd was still
enjoying being a crowd and he was displeased that they were
inhibiting his moment. Without taking them back to the

beginning, it was necessary to stop the action and resolve the problem. This we did, on suggestions from the crowd, by giving him a box to stand on and getting him to start his announcement with an arresting cry for attention. This brought him to the crowd's notice and let them know that the next phase of the action was imminent. For his announcement, and for the dance that followed, a certain amount of movement was necessary to clear sight-lines and to make space. However, once this point had been made and the cue given, numbers of children shot to their new positions as if by electrical impulse. We stopped again and naturalised the moment. After the dance, a fight was to develop, and here we had no problems about the uninhibited evacuation of areas. Then we stopped and took that bit through again. Some of them had forgotten some, but most had remembered most, of what we had done. Break arrived and was welcome. We had been working for an hour and a half.

After break, we started again. The children were fresher now and a number had used the break to work out new ideas for their parts. There was no question in their minds of being 'only one of the crowd'; they had a proper understanding of the importance of their scenes and of their contribution to them.

Later in the scene there was an important shift of attention from an attack on Pilgrim to Hopeful's protest about it. This took time because it was necessary to maintain the naturalness of the movement by avoiding any indication of preknowledge; initially, heads started to twitch round in anticipation of the cry of protest. By now, though, points were being taken readily and our only remaining problems were those of concentration and reactions. It is very disconcerting to see even one member of the cast gazing with interest at the audience instead of the other way round. It would be difficult for even the most accomplished Hamlet to maintain tension in the last act if just one courtier, however far Down Right, were slowly peeling and eating a banana. It was important for the children to realise that by their concentration on the action they enhanced it and, conversely, that a withdrawal of interest by only one person would diminish a performance. Sometimes, too, in the trial scene, some of them would forget their function and respond to the lines as audience rather than as performers, particularly when the lines were ones which, though funny, were supposed to be received with horror by the citizens. I pointed out that it is tedious to have to watch performers laughing at their own jokes – in reality as well as on television. However, by constant exhortation, by constantly mentioning what was good and what was not so that the children realised that their performances were really noticed, we achieved a crowd scene with which we were modestly satisfied.

The next morning, on the day of the first performance, we tied the whole thing together. The individual sections were ready and some of them pleased even the critical peers of the performers. There were some rather horrid gaps at times, when someone hadn't realised that his bit came next or had become so absorbed that he had forgotten it – or when, as happened once or twice, a short link between one section and another had not been written. They soon got used to improvising these where necessary. After we had gone through from beginning to end, we took the 'joins' in sequence, starting just before the end of one section, running through the link into the next section then stopping shortly after the beginning of it. After that, rehearsal became rather desultory. The Press came to take photographs, and in moving the 'tower' to the back of the hall in order to get far enough away to get all the cast in (in press photographs, the more faces, the more copies sold) they demolished one of the light fittings which lightened the mood for a while. Some children became so bored that they drifted back to their lessons. Others ran through bits, but rather mechanically now. Creation was over; performance was yet to come.

There are hundreds of different ways of tackling a production and it would be foolish to claim that any one approach is universally valid. A production must suit its own individual circumstances, but I feel that ideally a school production should meet the following requirements:

It should be essentially interesting or enjoyable for everyone concerned in it. Parents should not have to endure the experience of sitting through tedious and inept productions; the producer should not end up broken; the children should not be left with the feeling that they have lived through a singeing experience which has left them charred at the edges – though better that, in a way, than for them to have been ground down by relentless boredom. Consequently it is important for the children to be involved as far as possible in the creative processes of producing the play. This does not only mean that they should be actively involved in rehearsal instead of simply being told what to do and drilled into doing it, but that all the children, whether taking part or not, should be exposed to the ideas of the play and encouraged to contribute in many different ways – with dialogue if it is an original play, with ideas on interpretation and presentation, with setting and costumes, lighting and back-stage work. It is particularly important if the children are later to mount their own productions that numbers of them should have a good understanding of, and wide experience in, all the practical aspects of putting on a play – especially lighting. I always found, from the second year upwards, that there were children who were far more competent than I was at setting up and operating lighting for a production, given the required safeguards and supervision. All the players, even if not themselves technicians, should have some understanding of – and the greatest respect for – the work of those who, while not performing themselves, make the performances possible. They should also respect the work of others on the productions, however large or small a part they play. I could not do plays with crowds in if I did not believe that every individual member of the crowd was making a unique and valuable contribution to the production, nor could they themselves gain real satisfaction from what they were doing unless they also believed that.

Of course, some children have more to learn, or more to do, than others, and one of the things I always disliked was the

E

'prize' distribution of the leading parts. Consequently, in the end, I made this as random a process as possible, giving the parts to children who did not immediately come to mind as actors or actresses, and who could be relied on not to become spoiled by the experience. The precocious school child who is filled with admiration for his own performance is a horrid sight. Nor did the major parts inevitably go to one particular academic area – that would have been very wrong. I also tried to use not only the pleasantly conformist child but equally to find opportunities for the thorough nuisance who almost certainly needed the occupation and fulfilment of being involved in a play far more than the model child who would often be the immediate choice: not 'if you're not good you won't be in the play', but 'if you're not good, then you probably really need to be in it'.

In my last school I became used to working on large-cast plays, but the size of the cast is not the true criterion: the important thing is to use all those who want to take part – a dozen, two dozen, fifty, as the case may be. Selection can make the producer's job easier. It can give an extra dimension to the pleasure of those who have been selected. But it's not very pleasurable for those left out of the circle.

After the performances of *Transformation Scene*, one first year pupil wrote:

'On Monday morning I awoke very tired and, for some reason, unhappy. Why, I could not think. Monday is quite a good day for me, at least one which starts the week well. I usually awake quite happily. But today it was quite different. Today I was unhappy. Suddenly, it came to me – there would be no more rehearsals. It was over, finished.

For one week I had rehearsed, put all my effort into the play, but now it was over, finished with.

"All things come to an end. Life is not infinite. See, even this sunset light is passing and soon, before we realise it, the sunset will have become the sunrise and with the new day we shall be gone." This speech from the play seemed to fit the situation.

But this time the sun could not be tethered. This time it really was over.

I thought back to the times I had been rehearsing. The first time I knew I was to be in the play and how excited I was, but it was all over now, finished, done with. I wondered how the others who had been in the play felt. When I arrived at school I realised that all the people in my Tutor Group who had been in the play also felt the same way – even Alan who had helped with the lighting was sorry that it was over now.'

When I saw this in the magazine I was very pleased to see that he had understood what the play was about and had related the point to his own life. And I was interested to note that he wrote about the pleasure of the rehearsals, not of the performance.

Chapter 3

Music

I suppose the commonest relationship of Music with Drama is through productions: the play begins, and before any characters have appeared music can have firmly established the mood: sombre or gay, pastoral or foreboding. It is an immediately effective device. Later, perhaps, an angel delivers a not very interesting speech in a rather unconvincing way, but the backing of Vaughan Williams gives the scene an emotional impact far beyond that warranted by words or performance. In a tediously lengthy interval, well-amplified music relieves the boredom and helps to mask the heavy scuffling and altercations of the scene shifters. Using such instances as examples, a musician colleague once argued that Drama was parasitic, for it continually draws on other arts to enhance itself. It is a persuasive argument and one can readily understand the irritation of a musician who sees his art used merely to underpin a piece of drama. Music, my colleague held, was for writing, performing or listening to. Nothing else. I feel, though, that all the arts have something to offer each other.

There are many schools fortunate enough to have a well-founded music tradition, and for them it is no doubt relatively simple to mount *Let's Make an Opera* or Williamson's *Julius Caesar Jones* or even *Ruddigore*. We were not so fortunate, and the majority of our children did not really like or enjoy music – or, at least, that subdivision of music with which schools are more usually concerned. Their response to undemanding, rhythmic pop was as immediate as their withdrawal of interest from 'highbrow' music. Yet, if they had simply to *listen*, and keep still, they soon became fidgety and bored even by pop music. Admittedly, not as immediately or as intensely as when required to sit through one whole LP side of Beethoven, Berlioz

60

or Brahms, but nevertheless, bored. They felt like Lucy in *Peanuts*, that just listening to music was 'the most ridiculous thing I've ever heard!' Like her, they felt more natural when moving about to it, or singing bits of it, or dancing to it, or conducting it – anything, rather than just sitting. I am not saying that is how it should be: simply that this is how it was. However, I do not hold that 'listening; writing; performing' need necessarily be interpreted absolutely conventionally. Because the majority of our children did not enjoy involvement in music, except on some occasions when their interest was caught, I had to rely for a lot of the time on individual talents. When I wanted a song for our version of *The Snow Queen*, I had to ask the same second year boy who had done me a setting of Solveig's song for a previous *Peer Gynt* production. He was, at that time, the only one likely to produce one for me.

When the school first opened, though, this attitude to music had not developed, and my first venture in combining music and drama was one of the most satisfying. Very venturesome, too, we felt at that time, for it linked the work of three separate subjects. It was initiated by the Head of English who felt it would be interesting to produce what we called an opera, but which was in fact a play with a lot of songs. In the first year of the school's life, children of all abilities had produced a great deal of, generally, free verse. The suggestion was that for this particular project they should be encouraged also to write in regular verse patterns which would not give too much difficulty to anyone setting the words to music. They could, if they wished, set their own poems, or they could offer them for others to set. Enough children had the necessary technical knowledge to be able to compose and write down music.

The picaresque story line had been established in advance by the teachers concerned: Peter, the 'Dreaming Boy' of the title, is dissatisfied with the quiet life of his village and runs away, or perhaps dreams that he does. He goes to sea, is ship-wrecked, involved with gypsies, has a range of adventures and returns home (or wakes up) more appreciative of his placid life. This gave us a range of themes on which we could ask the children for verses. For instance, we first asked them for chants for self-invented children's games, with explanations of how they should be played. Here is the Stone Game, a version of the game 'Drop Handkerchief':

> Close your eyes, count one, two, three;
> The stone may come to you.
> If it does, then you'll be 'he'
> And we will start anew.

We opened the play with this and it proved so popular that we repeated it in the final scene. Later, we asked for sea shanties, songs for fairground vendors, farmers and so on. The most attractive combinations of words and music were included in the script, which I wrote; though, on reflection, it would have perhaps been better to have subdivided this into sections and encouraged the children to write at least part of it for themselves.

The performance was accompanied by one of the staff on the virginals. This unusual instrument was ideal for accompanying young children's voices as it sustained them without overwhelming them as a piano can sometimes do. The only instrumental contributions made by the children were a canon for recorders (composed almost casually by a first year pupil who is now teaching others to do likewise) and another for chime bars, representing with inappropriate, but attractive, lightness the sound of a big church bell. There was a brief interlude, too, for a raucous brass trio in the fair scene.

With such young children, we had problems of projecting immature singing voices in our large hall, despite the lightness of the accompaniment. Not so much with the choruses, the tunes of which carried robustly though the words were sometimes lost, but with the solo singers. Their voices had to carry but not show strain, and the words had to come over with meaning and personality. After all, an important part of this exercise had been the blending of words and music; words often made important commentary on the action, or helped to carry it forward. Sometimes, as in the sea shanties, one lost some of the pleasure if one didn't hear the words:

> (Part of a shanty)
> *Chorus*:
> Haul at the anchor, up and away.
> Haul at the anchor, up and away,
> Haul at the anchor, up and away,
> And off to sea we'll go.
>
> I met a girl in Port of Spain,
> With hair as black as pitch,
> But once she talked of marrying,
> I jumped into a ditch.
>
> *Chorus*:
> I found a girl in Trinidad
> And she was fat as butter
> But when she talked of wedding rings
> I jumped into the gutter.

Sometimes, too, it could be tedious for the audience to have to listen to an earnest child singing at some length without their having any idea of what he was singing about. Character also presented problems; those boys best trained to project their voices tended to be members of the church choir and their pure, impersonal tones were not always appropriate for bucolic farmers or swarthy gypsies, for example. We solved the problems, or most of them, eventually. Even those whose voices inconsiderately broke during the rehearsal period managed a sort of *sprechtstimme* worthy of (and, when they lost the melodic line, reminiscent of) Schoenberg's *Pierrot Lunaire*.

Later, at a time when there was little enthusiasm for music, I tried in starting 'Impetus' (q.v.), to put together a play incorporating music stolen from Schubert. I initiated a 'Composer's Concourse' (I quote the name with reluctance, but that was what we called it; at that time, somehow, names seemed very important) and one boy from my tutor group, with the help of another boy also working towards a Music O level, borrowed scores and started extracting the themes I had selected, and adapting them so that words could be set and sung to them. The idea offended some members of staff but gave pleasure to those working on the scheme.

However, the needs of *The Sword* came first and, that time at any rate, I was saved from sacrilege. I asked the Concourse to produce the music for our joint project. The boy from my tutor group was writing a symphony as part of his O-level work, supplementing his composition with a commentary on the composers who had influenced his writing of it, from the Haydnesque first movement, through Dvorak, Delius and Copland to last movement echoes of Shostokovich and Prokofiev. These in turn reflected the range of records I had been lending him, for he was an eclectic listener and composer. I therefore expected the music to be mildly derivative, echoing perhaps Bloch, perhaps Rimsky-Korsakov. However, I left the approach entirely to the boys who were doing the score. No songs were required; the need was solely for music to accompany the action. The 'Prologue' to the play, for instance, represented a blood sacrifice, and needed music which grew from a soft, sinister beginning to a climax as the dagger was raised and plunged into the victim. Provided they followed the required pattern, the form and content of their accompaniment was entirely their concern.

I heard the results with surprise. They were far more appropriate and evocative than anything I had envisaged. The three of them had first gathered together all the percussion instruments which were available in the school: chime bars, xylophones, bongos, kettle drums, side drums. To supplement these, they borrowed maraccas and tambourines and cymbals. They also had available a cello, a violin, the virginals, guitars and a zither. They set all this up in the music room late one evening so that the usual external noises of the daytime should not interfere with their taping. Then they experimented, trying combinations of instruments to see what kind of sound was produced.

They soon established two points: that the stringed instruments in fact sounded more appropriate to their purpose if deliberately played out of tune; and that the only valid way of evaluating the sounds produced was by listening to a play-back on the tape-recorder. Initially they wasted some time producing sound which excited them only to realise later that it made quite a different effect on the listener – or, in this instance, the microphone which represented him. Balance was an important factor; an effective accompaniment which seemed to the performer to maintain a good rhythmic impulse and also to create an interesting texture could be completely swamped, for instance, by an instrument placed nearer to the microphone. On the other hand, juggling the positions could, conversely, give importance to sounds which would normally not be heard against the others being produced.

Next, it became obvious that it was physically impossible for each to have access to the full range of instruments, so they divided their 'orchestra' into three. Now, they worked on rhythmic patterns, starting with the simple and moving on to the more complex. They found that, as with chamber music, someone had to take the lead, but they found also that rapport and intuitive response to each other was often more useful than any other means of indicating the tempo or the intensity of the sound. Part chamber music, part jazz, in fact. A long time was spent practising combinations of instruments, recording, discussing, amending. At last they felt ready to try one of the required pieces, and they started work on the background for the Prologue.

They chose this to begin with because the shape and length of the piece were dictated very largely by the action it was to accompany. From the various sound patterns they had experimented with they selected some which they felt would best establish the sinister mood of the opening. They tried various combinations of rhythmic patterns for the opening section and recorded a couple of minutes of these. Apart from some balance adjustments, they were satisfied with them. Next, they had to decide how to build up the climax, to agree on its impetus, its timing – and the sound which it should be conveyed in. After more experiments, they were ready to try this section on tape, too. After that, the whole piece was put together and recorded two or three times – never exactly the same, for there were always variations in tempo and instrumentation – deliberately so; they kept the whole thing flexible and improvised as the mood took them. After a number of attempts, they had two or three versions of 'Prologue' for the cast to choose from. Then they went on to a piece where sustained notes and texture were more important than rhythm. They approached this in the same way, so absorbed that they did not notice the dawn showing outside the steamed-up windows. When the caretaker started his early morning rounds they were still absorbed; but the gradual intrusion of extraneous noise brought the session to an end.

I wish I had been there, but I had no idea until afterwards of what they had in mind. If I had known, I think that, lacking experience, I would have doubted very much the value of such an experiment. However, the results proved otherwise: as soon as the cast heard the tapes, they wanted to start moving to them, speaking to them. They gave the production a tremendous lift. At this time, this sort of thing was completely new to me – to all of us, though we have since been exposed to the Avant Garde. I don't think I shall ever again feel quite the excitement of a new approach as when, expecting an innocuous piece of pastiche, I first heard these totally unexpected sounds.

Yet it was surprising how soon one accepted this particular approach and found uses for it in many ways. On one youth drama school, we found a battered piano, front missing, totally out of tune, derelict, apparently useless. But one group, who were developing a ritualistic piece of movement, taped one 'chord' with all its consequent janglings and overtones. They then made a loop of it and played it continuously through their scene with hypnotic effect. In Dance Drama work (q.v.), I mention how we experimented with unusual or home-made percussion instruments. Often, the less conventional were the more satisfying: a glass with marbles in it; large cardboard boxes which could be thrummed; pennies tapped and jingled. All manner of things can be shaken (pins in a tin, peas in a box), tapped (windows, ink-holder, covers, books, plastic sandwich boxes) drummed (chair seats, waste-paper bins). It is even possible to make one's own pottery rattle which makes a lovely sound: a shape with decorative holes in and a clay marble inside. And, as one almost inevitably uses these sounds taped, even normally insignificant sounds, like crumpling paper or the ticking of a watch, can be amplified into an interesting part of the overall texture, especially when balanced on a recording with more dominant sounds, more distantly recorded. Organisation is of course necessary, and the taped results are more likely to be satisfying, if like the backgrounds for *The Sword*, they follow a fairly lengthy period of just trying things out. On one youth drama school, we decided to experiment with home-devised percussion and set aside an afternoon session for this. Everyone gathered very promptly with lengths of tubing, boxes, tins, jars, sheets of cardboard, bins, milk bottles filled to different levels – an ingenious assortment. Spontaneously, the experimenting began. Rhythms were picked up, passed round, replaced by others. At one point, one 'instrument' would become dominant while the others accompanied; at other times, antiphonal effects were produced. Instead of taping it, I decided first to organise it, to formalise the procedure. As soon as I established a respectable pattern, the life went out of the exercise. I should have left it alone for much longer.

Just as making music can be interpreted in a number of ways, so, too, listening to music can mean many things. At its most unproductive, it can simply mean sitting still and quiet until a piece of music has worked its way through to the end. It can mean following a score, or following a verbal analysis. It can mean carrying on a conversation, occasionally breaking off to hum the more striking parts of a background record. It can, of course, mean just listening; but what else? Building images, comparing interpretations, following the composer's argument, visualising the situations or places portrayed in a piece, tapping out the rhythms with a Prom programme – there are many ways of listening, not one of them absolute. I would certainly argue that moving to music or, sometimes, writing to it can involve a child in more

67

purposeful listening than sitting mute and facing the record player. At the youth drama schools, we started each day with movement work and I tried them with a number of records, not only of peaceful works but sometimes of turbulent music. Once, I used the opening of the Sixth Symphony of Arnold Bax, grinding, uncompromising music, matched well by the movement of the youngsters. At one moment, there is a brief pause before the music starts again with increased urgency. At this moment, all movement ceased, everyone was still, poised, then, exactly matching the music, they plunged once more into powerful activity. The matching of movement and sound could not have happened without the most acute consciousness of the development of the music.

I frequently used music as a stimulus for writing. At first, I would get the children to listen, acutely, in a time of quietness in the classroom, then write about what they had heard:

> A plane rolling and rumbling like thunder;
> A class chattering away;
> A bird with a clear song;
> Our teacher whispering;
> A trolley being rolled along the pavement;
> Plastic being placed down roughly and hard;
> Inkwells going backwards and forwards;
> A scrubbing brush being rubbed –
> And the atmosphere in our class busy again.

Then, I would use music. When I first started, I was unnecessarily apprehensive about using 'abstract' music which could convey a mood but little more, and I used music which described characters, asking the children to re-create in words the people portrayed in, for instance, some of the 'Enigma' Variations ('Dorabella' particularly appealed to them) or in the second movement, 'Allegro commodio e flemmatico', of Nielsen's 'Four Temperaments' Symphony. ('He's never English,' said one girl. 'He's an easy-going Dutchman, wandering along the quayside.' That was near.) I also used music which told a simple story, though when I played one group the exciting part from the Tale of the Kalendar Prince from *Scheherezade*, they all burst out laughing. It was too melodramatic for them. After that, I always used music which appealed to me, feeling that if the material did not rouse my own enthusiasm, I would be unlikely in turn to be able to engage that of the children. Vaughan Williams' *Job*, of which I am very fond, received a much better reception. After listening to Job's Dream, one girl wrote:

Job's Dream

Hands reach out, loving hands, pale, slender,
They hold gently, moving, feeling, caressing.
Soft voices, high and slow,
Singing in some strange, beautiful language.
Cool winds brush past,
Carrying away fear, carrying away hate.
Rain falls, light, soft, pit-pat filling the air
As it falls on the dark rich ground.
Everything is blazed in soft warm sunlight . . .

Then come footsteps, thudding footsteps,
The sun seems to turn black,
Winds, return hard, angry,
Bringing back fear, bringing back hatred
Armies, millions of armies pour over the hills as one
    would pour water.
As they come, things wither, melt and die before
    them.

On and on they come.
Monotonous stamp, stamp, louder, louder.
The rain changes; it's long pointed, sharp,
Cutting through the ground, through trees.
The air changes;
It's hot, it's cold; snow storms, blazing sun.

Long arms, evil, covered with blood,
Dragging, pulling, heaving, nearer, nearer,
Breath hot, steaming, sticky.
Teeth grinning evil, hatred, spite.
Arms reaching, longing to kill.

Lightning flashes, streak after streak lights the sky.
Still it's hot, still it's cold.
Still the steady stamp, stamp, stamp, goes on, on, on . . .

There is less noise; no more lightning,
Fleeting glimpse of a red scaly arm,
Then darkness covers everything,
Peace returns. Fear vanquished.

There were always one or two 'groups' in any year: three or four boys with guitars, percussion and perhaps piano, very eager to play for discotheque sessions, school dances, or any other occasion. If opportunities arose for them to be used in a play, or in connection with one, this was always arranged on the understanding that they must not be amplified beyond the limits of endurance. For a mock melodrama, one such group supplied all the live music, accompanying silent film sequences, patriotic ballads, speciality acts, and finally forming the focus for a 'pre-massacre orgy'. For a musical version of *The Taming of the Shrew*, we stole tunes from Norwegian folk songs, which were very jolly and much enjoyed. We did also have one or two individual compositions. The one which was undoubtedly (and deservedly) the most popular was 'written' by a boy who in fact had no knowledge of musical notation. He had a very good ear, though, and devised both melody and accompaniment by constant trial and error on the piano. The result was very successful and might well not have been so had it been reached by more conventional means. It certainly involved a great deal of painstaking effort. It would not, for instance, have been a suitable method for producing all the music for *The Dreaming Boy*.

Although, after the first year, few of our children were technically equipped to read or write music, we nevertheless managed to evolve a folk opera, *Aftermath*, with original music produced by the children. We used the word 'folk' in talking of the work in a deliberate, and successful, attempt to give it a popular image. From the beginning, we planned to use a group to accompany it, and the whole enterprise gained much impetus from the enthusiasm for folk music, which was considerable at that time.

The main problem, of how to get music written or devised by children who could not follow musical notation, was ingeniously dealt with by the Music specialist. She selected some classes and arranged that the children should work in pairs. One from each pair then made up and sang a musical phrase to the other. This involved a lot of singing and la-ing because the phrase had to be well memorised or there would be no record of it. If they had all had access to tape recorders, perhaps that part of the exercise would have been easier. However, although the noise was considerable and therefore distracting to some, all the pairs managed to produce not only the first phrase but also the second stage of the process, an answering, complementary phrase from the second person. They then memorised the two phrases. They could also call on the teacher at any time to write down an elusive phrase or for technical advice when they knew what they wanted to produce but could not quite manage it. From time to time, they all stopped and listened to what the other pairs had produced. Sometimes, helpful criticism led to an amendment. Sometimes, it would be pointed out that the tune had been written before, although it might neverthless develop individually. The process was then continued until a complete tune had been assembled by each pair. Writing the tunes down had to be the job of the teacher and this took a lot of time, though not all the tunes were finally written down, for one reason or another. When I heard the tunes, I sometimes found it difficult to realise how they had been arrived at; their 'A,B' origins were not obvious.

Some of the pairs set words to their tunes, others left this to me. I had a tape of the most likely tunes and, having selected the ones which seemed most attractive and most amenable to being set to words, I started the slow business of fitting words and tune together.

When we came to performance, we found ourselves up against the usual practical problems. The voices were at first completely inaudible when matched, this time, not against virginals but against a group very proud of its amplifying equipment. This problem was never fully resolved. I find it impossible to agree with guitarists on the amount of amplification which is acceptable, desirable, or even tolerable. However, we allowed them to play very loudly indeed when people weren't singing. We used unamplified guitars to accompany the lighter voices, or had them singing unaccompanied when we felt confident that they could sustain the melodic line without support. Once or twice, a singer was able to accompany himself with a few simple chords, and if I ever did it again I would not have the accompaniment performed by a separate group but by performers on the acting area. One song, accompanied by a thrumming guitar played by one of the singers, had been composed by the children who sang it. At one rehearsal, they came up and said, 'We've got a song', and tried it out for us. It was so simple – in fact, it looks banal, written down. But sung with involvement and feeling by the boys who devised it was a moving personal statement.

Somehow, because of the division which they had erected between categories of music – and which we had allowed to remain – they did not think of this sort of thing as 'real' music. Their reason for this was, I fear, that this kind of thing gave them pleasure, which was something they did not expect from what they regard as the Establishment subject. Once I was involved in an 'integrated situation', an important-sounding term which simply meant that I did not have to keep strictly within the bounds of my own subject (if they could be identified, that is) but could use the resources of other subjects, notably PE and music. In other words, what I normally did, but now made respectable by use of the appropriate terms. If I had said:

'Right, now we will explore our theme through the medium of music', they would have groaned and felt deprived. Instead, we simply explored our theme, not isolating our media. One group worked all the time with electronic music, listening, selecting, moving to it. Another made their own sounds with conventional percussion instruments borrowed from the music room, supplemented by home-made instruments. Others picked out music on the piano, devising a tune for their scene. Others, in search of national music to indicate different areas visited, listened with serious concentration to Dvořák, Sibelius, Nielsen, Tchaikovsky, Schubert. The reality of the situation was, to my mind, more important than definitions of it.

There is undoubted value in writing, creating, devising your own music, and a piece of Drama is often a useful vehicle for presenting it. At least then, if you are 'using' music, you are making use of your own creation, interpreted by yourself or your contemporaries. Nowadays, music suffers less from excessively narrow definitions. Where there is a vital music tradition, Youth Orchestras, groups of instrumentalists, singers, young composers working not only traditionally but also experimentally, definitions don't really matter. Music is alive and growing, and that is the important thing. But when it is not, then a narrow view could finish it for good: singing means the choir and 'Nymphs and Shepherds', but never the Beatles; playing means the recorder or the piano, but not mouth organ or milk bottles; composing means harmony, counterpoint, and key signatures, but not exploring sound. As definitions, arguable; as epitaph, regrettable.

F

Chapter 4

Filming

I did my first piece of film work with a class almost immediately after I bought my first ciné camera. It was a Standard 8 mm which took cassettes containing thirty-three feet of film, an unusual camera which cost me very little, but when I learned to use it gave me very good service. At that time I was by no means sure how to handle it, but balanced my lack of knowledge with considerable enthusiasm. I made the film with a senior class who had proved particularly difficult to involve in work which I considered purposeful. At first, the reaction was one of excitement and pleasure: to make a film was a distinct novelty and carried a certain cachet. But it was never finished; the enthusiasm died, and the cast started to leave. Still, I learned a lot.

It seemed a good idea to build the film on a play which the class had made as a joint effort. The plot was complicated but exciting, based on a robbery, with lots of violence. The first scene, showing the robbers plotting their crime, had taken place in a cafeteria. However, we found that there was not enough light indoors. Besides, the classroom did not provide a sufficiently neutral background. So it became an outside café. The sun was shining brightly, but it was very blowy and rather cold; so, as the cast knew all the details of the action, we aimed to start filming immediately. I set the lens aperture according to the film-maker's instructions, looked through the viewfinder and called to the actors to start. Part of the dramatic tension in the original scene had come from the fact that the robbers had at various times had to break off their conversation because one of the cafeteria staff came near them while clearing up the tables. In this 'outside' version, we had decided that this clearer-up had to be promoted to waiter, but his basic function was the same. However, the boy playing the part, called Smiler by his contemporaries because of his light-hearted disposition, began to expand his part, interpolating various extra pieces of action such as flicking the table with a handkerchief, laboriously licking a pencil and writing down the order, crossing it out and so on. This irritated not only the other performers but also the rest of the class, who were getting cold. It was not really effective film material either, because I was standing well back in order to get all the action in, so the subtleties of his performance did not come over.

One disadvantage of having to look through a view-finder is that one cannot at the same time watch a group who are becoming increasingly bored and finding other activities to interest them. However, at this point one boy, whose contribution to the play had been to produce a very effective diagram of the planned robbery for use in this scene, suggested that his diagram should be shown, close-up, with fingers pointing out particular aspects of the plan. This seemed a good idea, so we moved in close to the table. The break enabled me to call the class to order and it also temporarily ended the waiter's interpolations. The robbers were not very happy about this, because they had not been able to complete the dialogue of this particular scene. But, as the others pointed out, as it was a silent film, the dialogue was not really necessary.

By now, everyone was rather cold and irritable. However, we took a shot of the diagram with fingers moving about on it. The waiter's finger appeared at one point, but I didn't recognise it through the view-finder and refused to take the shot again, pointing out that if I hadn't recognised it, no one else would. I then retired, with the rest of the class, to shoot the rest of the scene from a distance. The waiter came up with the bill and must have passed some remark, for one of the robbers hit him suddenly, providing a most effective, though unpremeditated, sequence. Shortly afterwards, the camera stopped and I assumed that the cassette had run out. I had yet to learn that one must wind a spring-operated camera. We returned to the classroom to get warm. By now, we had used up most of the period, a lot of it spent arguing. Still, the film was packed up ready for sending off, and this re-animated enthusiasm: the thought of 'seeing ourselves' is a powerful attraction and still redeems a lot of home movies.

But next week the film had not been returned and it was impossible to persuade them to continue the shooting until they had seen their first results. The week after, when they did, their disappointment was intense. Purely by luck the film had been correctly exposed and the images were sharp, but the class complained that they couldn't really see anything. At the time, their complaints seemed most ungrateful, but I now understand their disappointment. To begin with, film to them meant the sort of thing you see in a cinema or, more frequently, on a tele-vision screen. Film meant size and clarity and an 8-mm projector in an inadequately blacked-out hut produced not a good, large, clear picture but a small one which they had to crowd round and peer at. Moreover, I had compounded the problem by standing so far away to film the action that the tiny figures did not really have a chance to convey much. The diagram was far more effective and the boy who drew it was justifiably proud. The moving fingers raised a laugh, but it was generally agreed that the one shot had conveyed far more than all the rest, for the tedium of which they were inclined to blame Smiler – a little unjustly, for despite his irritating additions to the plot he had at least been more animated than the robbers, who had merely conversed.

They were all intrigued by the considerable quantity of black, unexposed film and when I explained what had happened, for the humanity of my mistake they forgave me much. They watched the film through again, though it plainly bored them. The black film had really caught their interest, though. Someone asked if he could handle some of it. There were a lot away that day, so I was able to divide the unexposed film up so as to give each group of four or five quite a reasonable length. For a while, they simply enjoyed handling it, then they found that scratching the dull side produced a different result from scratching the shiny one – the dull, emulsion, surface could be scraped away. With pins, knives, compass points, finger nails, they scratched. Then one group decided to try to draw their own pictures by scratching. At first, they drew large images which would have covered several frames, then they compared them with the, to them, miniscule frames of the film we had taken. That group then simplified their images, trying to relate them to the frame size. Others, less patient, scratched pretty well at random. Next they wanted to see the results. I spliced some of the pieces into loops and ran these through the projector. They roused considerable enthusiasm, particularly as the continuity of the loop enabled them to study specific points at frequent intervals. The lesson passed quickly. They wanted to keep their pieces of film, and this seemed reasonable – indeed, next week, two of the loops were produced again and showed evidence of considerable work and thought. One group had experimented with added colour, using, I think, coloured Indian ink, and the results were vital and attractive. A number of them would like to have continued with this work, but I had no more black film left, and in any case we had started a story film and I felt that it should be finished.

So we carried on, week by week, filming when the weather was suitable, generally only for part of a lesson, because those not directly involved quickly, and with reason, became bored. I decided fairly early on that it was necessary to have someone else doing the camera work to leave me free to keep an eye on the class. I gave one of the boys a quick course of instruction on which viewfinder to look through and which button to press, and he managed very well. He was very pleased and proud at this responsibility. On one occasion, we had another class in with us and showed them the film as far as we had got with it – I had spliced the various bits together. They were uncomplimentary and complained not only of the technical short-comings but also of the obscurity of the story line. Half the time, they said, they couldn't understand anything that was happening. They suggested that the use of interpolated titles would have helped, and they commented pointedly on the way the characters seemed to change costume, even during the course of one sequence. This was a valid point, for the cast's clothing, although basically the same from week to week, did tend to vary considerably in detail. Colour seemed to matter less than variation in pattern or style. Sometimes, we would take the first part of a sequence with one of the characters wearing a plain shirt and the next week he would appear in a boldly-checked one, reminiscent of the Canadian backwoods. The class defended the film, but more out of loyalty than conviction.

We plodded on, making more and more concessions to circumstances and enjoying the exercise less and less. At the end of the term, a lot of the class left and the remainder were amalgamated with another class. Thankfully, we abandoned the film and no-one mentioned it again. I was left pondering the fact that an idea which had started as a specially exciting stimulus should have finished up such a bore, and that something which I had intended as a creative exercise should have degenerated into something so uninspired and pedestrian. Also, the only really creative part of the whole exercise had been when they themselves handled and experimented with the film.

However, I did later make other films in class time and the circumstances – and the quality of the films – improved. There were certain problems which remained extremely difficult to overcome, such as that of the full involvement of the entire group. I was surprised how much extra concentration was achieved by supplying everyone with a 'viewer' made by cutting a rectangle from a piece of card. They watched the action through this and so got a somewhat clearer idea of what was actually being taken. Our normal vision is so 'wide-angled' that it is sometimes difficult to visualise what the more restricted camera is seeing and recording. Some groups were more taken with the technicalities than others, but the making of each film was prefaced by enough technical instruction to enable everyone to follow what was being done in the shooting of a sequence.

We learned a number of other things, too; that one could film out of sequence and cut the film about, for instance. Per-

haps this may seem overwhelmingly obvious, but it did not at
first appear so to the children, or to me. When they realised
this, they became excited by the possibilities it opened up. At
its simplest, it meant that if we had left an outdoor sequence
unfinished one week and it was raining the next week, then we
could simply turn our attention to another, indoor sequence,
especially as we soon acquired some inexpensive indoor lighting
equipment which proved invaluable. But the implications went
far deeper than this. We realised that we could alter the whole
emphasis of a scene by 'cutting-in' a shot taken at another
time. For example: a man has broken into a house and is
searching it. Now, if one cuts in a shot of someone else approaching the front door, the mood of that original scene is intensified
in a particular way. The effect is quite different if one cuts in
a shot of a dead body in the room which the intruder is approaching; or if one interpolates a shot of a bowl of custard
propped insecurely on top of a partly-open door which he is
about to go through; or if the cut-in shot shows that the rest
of the house behind the door has collapsed with the cliff on
which it stands – a shot we unfortunately never got round to
taking.

Being able to cut and re-arrange the film meant that the
finished result did not have to show what actually happened,
but merely what appeared to happen. In one film we made
about an escape from a prisoner of war camp, a prisoner had to
run across a roof and jump on to a unsuspecting guard below.

1. Prisoner runs across the roof. (This shot, taken from ground
level, effectively silhouetted the prisoner against the skyline.)
2. Guard coming through archway below.
3. Prisoner jumps to edge of the roof. Cut in mid-jump.
4. Prisoner jumps through the air. (For this, the boy playing
the prisoner stood on a step ladder, the cameraman lay on the
floor. The steps were not visible in the shot, only the prisoner,
who jumped over the camera. We took this at twenty-four
frames a second, to extend it.)
5. Below, the guard moves into view and the prisoner jumps

into the picture, landing on the guard's back and bringing him to the ground. (For this, the prisoner stood by the cameraman, rather insecurely, on top of a step-ladder, at the beginning of the shot. Then, as the guard moved into the picture, the prisoner jumped down on to him with effective, though unnecessary, heaviness.)

The whole sequence took quite a time to take, though it is over very quickly in the film. It also took a lot of careful cutting and editing, but the result was well worth it and drew a real-live gasp from its first adult audience. The children who made it hugged themselves with delight. It really did look a highly perilous piece of action. We learned later that the first shot had been potentially the most perilous: the roof was unsafe.

We had already learned to keep the narrative line simple, especially since our films were silent, with music or commentary added later. We learned, too, that a very considerable amount of work and time went into a film which might last no longer than five or ten minutes (some of our marathon twenty-minute efforts lacked the clarity and economy of many shorter films); and that a film could as effectively convey a mood or a feeling as a story: it didn't have to be a straightforward piece of narrative. Another useful device was to divide the time spent on filming, so that some of it was done in class, involving all or most of the pupils, the rest, involving two or three volunteers, being done on Saturdays. The out-of-school sequences were thoroughly discussed first in class time, and anyone who cared to come and watch the actual filming was welcome to do so. In our film, *The Escape*, the camp sequences were taken with the full class in lesson time, and those specifically concerning the escapers on two Saturday afternoons. For this film, we made use of a limited wardrobe of clothing, helmets, capes and so on, which we collected together for this particular purpose, thus saving a lot of trouble with continuity. By this time, too, I had made it clear that we were not settling to a film show when the sequences were returned from processing, but viewing and evaluating the 'rushes'. A little dabbling in terminology helps a lot. We also found that the discussion greatly helped the team of volunteer editors, who cut, arranged and spliced the sequences after school. The actual job of editing was not a profitable one for the whole class, but the consideration and evaluation could be.

I found that I had moved more and more towards the group-devised film, and this considerably helped involvement at all stages. For *The Escape*, for instance, the starting point came early in a class discussion with a vital, non-conforming group of fourteen-year-old secondary modern boys. My introductory remarks had included the fact that practical reasons required that the in-school filming take place on the premises, but this did not necessarily pre-suppose a school-based story, for subtle and imaginative use of various aspects of the buildings could suggest other environments. From one boy's sardonic comment, 'a prison camp, for instance', the story of the film grew.

The process of development was one which by now had become pretty well standard: first, a general story line was agreed. This involved a great deal of animated discussion as it was developed and amended, and took up not only the Drama period but also the one following it. By the end of the two periods, we had arrived at a story which, as was subsequently pointed out to us, bore a marked resemblance to the 'Wooden Horse' story, though we really had been unaware of this – we felt we had produced something exciting and original. After this, we broke the whole plot down into a series of sequences and fully discussed each sequence before we filmed it. Whenever possible someone – generally me – produced a duplicated 'story board' of the sequence before we filmed it, so that each member of the class who had already contributed at the discussion stage had, as it were, visual minutes of the discussion. When the actual shooting was taking place, anyone not in the shot could comment on the trial runs, on expression, on performance, pace, timing, and so on; and they did, forthrightly. It was accepted, however, that only the cameraman could actually see what would appear on the screen, so his opinion carried most weight. This way, we produced a film in which all the members of the class felt actively involved and to which they had all contributed ideas and enthusiasm as well as performances. It was a great stimulus for oral communication, our silent film.

By this time, I had learned the importance of letting others see the film as far as it had gone and of listening to their comments. You know, when you have made a film, what you intended to convey; but only others can tell you whether you have succeeded in conveying it. I have always found it very hard to curtail – or to dispense with – shots of which I have become fond, even though they may add nothing to the over-all effect of the film – may, indeed, detract from it.

Further experience taught me more about resourceful use of available backgrounds. At its simplest, it meant a neutral grey wall which was often used as the background for numerous 'interiors' (which appeared, on occasion, noticeably draughty); but imaginative use of resources could produce the most interesting results. For instance, a shot through a window which, because it faced the playground, was covered with wire netting, produced a most atmospheric shot early in *The Escape*. The playground itself, taken from the roof of the school, made a blank, grey background, also useful in that film, but particularly effective in another film which represented happenings after death. The pillars in the central courtyard of one school were used to suggest a number of different settings.

Much of the essential background to the filming was conveyed in the invaluable study extracts from the British Film Institute, which the class enjoyed greatly, and discussed extensively, learning much from them. They could certainly learn far more about the art of directing and the technique of editing from a consideration of the Odessa Steps sequence from *The Battle-ship Potemkin* than they could from listening to me talking. I frequently used examples of good film, in the form of study extracts and shorts in class time, and we also ran a Film Society which was very popular though financially precarious. We balanced one expensive film against cheap or free-loan films each season. In this way the children saw a fair number of masterly silent films, such as those of Lloyd and Keaton, which were remarkably cheap to hire. They loved them, and learned a lot from them.

When more cameras were available, it was possible to arrange group filming in class time, as, for instance, in this session with a class of mixed second year comprehensive children.

I had started by outlining the sort of 'visual anecdote' I thought we should aim for: not an extended exercise, but something easily finished in two or three single periods. The children then divided up into groups of their own choosing. The lessons took place in a hut, so they could make plenty of noise without arousing peeved comments from next door or below. (Not that such comments were common – the rest of the staff being used to, perhaps resigned to, Drama sessions.) The children had no previous experience of filming, but their first task was to develop a simple story line and then to work out how best to convey the visual impression of this to the rest of the class. They knew that they had to make their point without the aid of the spoken word, but in presenting their ideas to the class they could use any means to make their impression clearly and effectively. The discussion of plot and presentation took one period plus varying amounts of individual time.

It was early in the summer term, In one group of four boys, two had become much interested in, and quite proficient at, throwing the javelin. A cinematic record of their prowess would, they felt, be of value.

. . . 'but that would be boring,' came the objection, 'just seeing you throw the javelin'. The discussion roamed into personal exchanges. 'Well,' said the javelin advocates, 'if you don't like it, then someone suggest something better.' In the presence of a dominating idea, forcefully presented, this is not always easy. No other suggestion came, but the objection that the javelin idea would be boring was renewed. 'Not if we hit someone with it.' This was intended as a jocular reply, but it produced a real response and awakened interest. Very soon they established, with some reluctance, that they would not be able to *show* someone being impaled, but would have to *suggest* it.

Who would be the most suitable recipient? That it should be the teacher organising the event met with immediate approval. So now they had an idea. This, they had to turn into a short story, with interest, tension, shape and point.

Next week, they presented the complete idea to the rest of the class. Sometimes groups would rely on straight narration, sometimes on a sort of moving tableau technique, or they would prepare large story-board-type illustrations done with a felt pen on sugar paper. (An overhead projector would have helped a lot here.) This group used narration supplemented by mime, roughly like this:

Well, there's a javelin contest and there's these three boys going in for it. Two of them are real toughs, brilliant javelin throwers . . . (the two javelin throwers prance about, looking very proud and bowing to the applause of the crowd) . . . and the third one is a real wet – an absolute drip. (One of the non-javelin boys shambles on, eliciting laughter from the boys, sympathy from the girls.) . . . Right. Number one throws and the crowd all goes . . . (He shades his eyes and appears to follow the impossibly long flight of the javelin, his head moving in an arc, with a slight jerk indicating that the javelin has landed. Then he jumps about, cheering and waving his arms.) The first thrower looks all smug . . . (The boy preens.) Then, the second one comes up, and it goes just the same. He throws . . . the crowd goes . . . and *he* looks all smug, too. Right. Up comes the third one. He staggers up to the line. (The boy lurches exhaustedly towards an imaginary throwing line.) He can just about lift the javelin to throw it . . . (This, too, he does, very feebly) . . . and the crowd all go . . . (The narrator starts to boo and jeer, then suddenly his expression changes to one of incredulity, then delight.) And he's got the teacher! So *he* looks all smug. And they all cheer him, and he's won the competition.

The rest were very taken with this anecdote and wanted to start on it straight away. So once again we found ourselves making a class film. There were a couple of points raised: firstly, how did he 'get' the teacher? A few irreverent suggestions, then the group's solution: make the body lie on the ground with the javelin apparently stuck right into him, but in fact held between the far side and the arm. Simple, but as it proved, effective. Secondly, how would the audience know that there was a competition on? The group had felt that anyone seeing the film would automatically assume this, but the rest of the class doubted it. The solution was to open with a shot of a silver cup on a table with a notice by it saying 'Grand Javelin-Throwing Competition'. Then, the film could be neatly rounded off with the winner being presented with the cup. We shot the film in a period and a half and would have been quicker had the cameraman not proved so easily moved to laughter. He was convulsed by some of the shots, vibrating the camera considerably, despite the fact that it was on a tripod. I was satisfied with my own performance.

There is some danger that the sheer novelty of making a film may be considered an end in itself. Although filming is increasingly popular now and at most beauty spots one can find several people admiring the scenery through the viewfinder of a camera, one can often still detect a note of automatic respect in response to the casual remark, 'We're making another film.' Film-making tends to be labelled progressive, adventurous and stimulating almost automatically. If one accepts this dictum uncritically, there is the distinct possibility that, while thinking that one is showing all these laudable traits, one may in fact be working in a dull, unimaginative and depressing way.

Two points need considering: how far should the control of the film be in the teacher's hands; and should all the class be involved all the time in all the aspects of making the film? It is not easy to defend the situation in which an only partially comprehending child is put in front of a camera operated by the teacher, and told by the teacher just what he must do; though it is perfectly possible to produce an effective film this way, especially with astute editing. But then, the child will really have gained very little beyond the simple pleasure most of us get when we see ourselves on a screen. He will not have been involved in the thinking, the discussing, the creating, the evaluating. So, simply making a film without the full involvement of all the children at all stages could be considered a pretty sterile exercise.

This televisually orientated generation has a fair intuitive understanding of the techniques involved in presenting a narrative in visual terms and this often shows in other aspects of their Drama works: their scripts and improvisations make much use of the flexibility in presenting a story which the influences of film and television have helped us to rediscover. The children are quick to grasp the basic essentials of film-making, including the technicalities. One instance: I felt pretty adventurous and liberal when I handed over the camera and light-meter to one twelve-year-old, but when I saw his immediate understanding and competence – he has since taken up a career in electronics – I began to feel that in fact I could quite possibly learn from him. When I saw the results he had produced I realised, too, that not only were they technically impeccable but that he showed that he had an acute perception of the visual effectiveness of a shot.

But just letting them do a lot to help you to make your film is again not enough. The full value of the exercise arises from fullest possible participation at all stages. This leads to difficulties in making a class film. I have indicated the various devices by which I tried to overcome the problem of having a few people actively concerned and a lot indifferently observing. The idea of a film can be a considerable stimulus to all sorts of oral work and discussion; it can lead to a critical assessment not only of one's own results but also, by comparison, of other film and television work; it can be a useful exercise in developing an idea and presenting it effectively within the particular disciplines of an art form; it can be great fun. But is the class the most efficient unit for this? There is certainly a case to be made for the class film. Sometimes it may be the only way in which a teacher can operate, and sometimes it can be an invaluable initial stimulus and shared experience. But one would hope it would develop from that so that children would automatically come to consider film as another medium for them to use: sometimes prose, sometimes painting, sometimes model, sometimes film. The really exciting culmination of this sort of work is when a group comes and says: 'We have an idea for a film, we want to make it, and can we borrow the Stuff?' One has to accept the fact that not every result will be successful, that there will sometimes be anxiety about the safety of expensive equipment, and some safeguards necessary, that some excellent work may never be finished. And of course, especially with the less responsible, one has to exercise discretion over supervision and assistance.

Out-of-school filming with a small, involved group did not present the organisational problems of class filming. Films came about in different ways. Sometimes, a setting would suggest a story: a quarry sparked off a story involving the rescue of someone stuck half-way up one of its sides; work on children's games suggested a film about the child who was always left out of everything; a child's face peering out of the window at the back of a van, led to one about a kidnapping. One remark, 'I wish I was invisible,' suggested a trick film about an invisible boy. A 'remarkably adult idea', to quote from the comment which accompanied its award in a national competition, developed from another remark, that dying must be 'like feeling things closing in on you'. A simple film, no story, simply a mood: a boy climbing a tree on a mist-heavy autumn afternoon; he falls; camera moves in to his face, picture dissolves into a grey blur; on a wide, open, neutral grey background he rises from a sprawled position; against a grey sky, he moves forward; gradually, he finds himself in a maze of pillars; less and less able to move freely; then, facing a blank wall, turning quickly away to find another behind him; on all sides, walls, closing in; one hand gropes up the wall; the hand lurches, swings, then hangs down; we see that it hangs from the side of a covered stretcher, which is carried off into the dusk.

87

This film was done with a small group. The first idea grew into an outline, then we resolved the technical difficulties of each shot as we came to it. The editing, done as a joint exercise, was particularly interesting, giving the whole film a shape and rhythm. Like many of the more fruitful filming experiences, this one arose in a non-structured situation and developed organically. Sometimes, especially with small groups, saying, 'Right, we're going to make a film, what shall we make it about?' effectively inhibits all further development, whereas chatting over all sorts of ideas would almost invariably lead, once a group had filming experience, to a consideration of the filmic possibilities of one or more.

One of my most rewarding experiences in this sphere, though, arose from the sort of remark which I have just abjured as inhibiting: to start off the idea of individual groups of filmers, I said to various classes of twelve-year-old comprehensive-school children that anyone who wanted to make a film could, provided he produced a good idea. Remarkably soon, one collection, all boys, arrived with a very full treatment of a story which they called *The Spy – Mr X*. They had no previous experience of filming, but they had lively imaginations, and one or two of them had distinct technical ability. One, who had a quite remarkable understanding of the medium, was elected director, and carried the full, detailed shooting script in his head. There was no written script, but he knew exactly how the story-line was to be developed and took endless trouble over each shot, first visualising it clearly, then translating that image into actuality. They needed a villain, and offered the part to me. It was a large and important part, though part of the idea was that the villain's face should not be seen until the last shot – of the villain being trundled away in a wheelbarrow. To ensure immediate identification, I was to have a tattoo mark, of a snake, on the back of one hand, and I was to wear a large riding mac in all shots. It was a gloriously warm summer, that year.

It was a very illuminating experience working with a director who knew exactly what he wanted and was going to get it. We

filmed on Saturdays and during Half Terms. The finished film
lasted about twenty minutes, but it took months to complete,
not because of indecision or lack of preparation but because of
a meticulous determination to get each shot exactly as the
director wanted it. He was certainly lucky with the weather –
it remained consistent whenever he was filming, which really
is unusual over such a length of time. He also ensured continuity by insisting that everyone had a special costume,
usually a particular pair of jeans, a particular shirt, just for the
film. All the performers and technicians were his personal
friends, so they had jointly discussed the plot through all its
stages and they continued this full communication of ideas,
sequence by sequence, before, during and after the filming. This
meant that they hardly wasted a foot of film, though I felt at
times they wasted some breath. Two sequences were, in my
view, a bit of a waste – an endlessly long shot, opening the film,
of the train supposedly bringing the villain to the town, and
a sequence in a wood, which was really underexposed and
hinged on a 'wanted' notice improbably pinned on a remote
tree. However, I had to remember that I was only a lay figure
(generally seen galloping away through a sunlit scene wearing
my stifling mac), and that, if this was to be their film, then it
wasn't my place to keep on interfering. One particularly hot
afternoon, after a good many trial runs at a particularly ener-
getic sequence, I delivered a strong lecture to one of the cast
who kept carping about the way in which we were doing it and
wanted to try another way. 'The director is the one who says
what goes,' I told him, 'and it's up to him.' 'No,' said the
director with irritating reasonableness, 'he's got a point there;
we'll try it his way.' We did, and it was indeed better his way;
though that was small consolation for another set of trial runs,
till we got it right the new way.

I'm not saying this was the only way to make films, or
indeed, that all groups were as competent or perceptive as
this one, but I do think this was probably the most useful
piece of film work I've been involved in. Partly, circum-

stances made it so. A close-knit group of friends who all knew what they were about and had a firm and positive notion of how they were going to put their ideas into effect minimised the danger of the situation becoming teacher-dominated. The teacher has the knowledge, experience and authority and can easily be the dominant factor in the out-of-school film despite a wish not to be. The children will not always be, initially, so fluent, so competent, so effective; the child-director may constantly turn to the attendant teacher for support, and it can happen – I've done it myself – that the teacher simply controls and directs the film through the child-director: he pulls the strings. Obviously, I'm not saying that there is no value in the children's taking part in the teacher's own film – again, I've done plenty of this myself – but the fullest value lies in the fullest experience. In the early stages it may be difficult, but ultimately one can reach a situation in which senior pupils, especially, readily initiate and carry out their own projects.

Films need not always tell a story: this could be inhibiting. They can simply be chronicles of events such as important happenings in the school year, or the life of the town, for instance; or a chronicle of the development and life of the neighbourhood, perhaps mixing diagrams and animated sequences in with 'live' film; or various forms of animated film (cartoon, puppet, flowers unfolding to the light); or just an abstract sequence on images. One lovely, fresh film was made very simply by a group who used circus paintings and animated cut-outs of clowns and animals. And so on. It's easy to think of film only in the more conventional sense, but why shouldn't one try to illustrate a pop record with moving images? Or present an aspect of history? Or draw on a film? One can see that filming need not necessarily be a group activity. It is possible, and often valuable, for an individual to comment in film on a theme that interests him, and it would be heartening to see this becoming more common. Of course, there is the question of expense, but there's a tendency to over-emphasise this: there is plenty of very good second-hand and superseded equipment available very reasonably, certainly more reasonably than a lot of much more common apparatus. And if one does one's own developing, running costs work out cheaper than many people realise, especially if one involves the active interest of the Science specialists.

I have deliberately not attempted in this chapter to give instruction in the techniques of film-making; that is properly material for full, specialist books on the subject. Obviously, it is very important to have the technical knowledge; it saves a lot of wasted time, effort and money. But on the non-technical aspects of filming, it is valuable to remember that, although rules are important, they are not sacrosant. For instance, I was conditioned to avoid the jump-cut; but came the New Wave, and that and lots of my other rules of thumb needed re-assessing.

It will be obvious that, though I have reservations about the total value of class filming, I have given attention to it not only in this chapter but also in my own experience. At first, the class film seemed the natural way of going about it, but now, fortunately, with an increase in flexibility arising from inter-disciplinary work, team-teaching situations, and a greater emphasis on individual or group work, the opportunities for freer use of film work are growing. Although I feel safer when working to a preconceived pattern and plodding peacefully from one expected situation to another, I nevertheless find that the sudden arrival of the unexpected is usually a valuable stimulus for thought and reconsideration.

Chapter 5

Playwriting

The children naturally wrote a lot of dialogue. Sometimes, they wished to give more permanence to a piece of work which had started as an improvisation. At other times, it made a change from improvised work, though often a group script would be approached through some kind of improvisation. For instance, a group would sit round and try out lines for inclusion in a scene whose overall pattern had already been agreed by discussion, each child taking the part of a predetermined character, with agreement already established on that character's nature and function. The lines themselves would then be further discussed, amended, polished, then written down. Another way was to tape-record a piece of work, then for the group, or sometimes one or two volunteers, to go through it, developing and turning it into a full written script.

Occasionally, one child or group of children would produce an original script just for pleasure or interest. Generally, these suffered from two major drawbacks. Because the children found it hard to plan, sustain and develop dialogue, it tended to be thin, moving jerkily from one hard pellet of information, lacking subtlety, fluency and naturalness. In any case, it was far too brief for practical purposes. For instance:

ACT TWO. *The same night. When the curtain is up, scene is in darkness. Suddenly, there is a pistol shot from off-stage.*
Mr M (*off*) Arggh.
The cast run downstairs. Lights are put on.

Lady S	Oh my God! What is it?
Lord S	There, never mind, dear.
Mrs S	It sounded like a pistol shot.
Mrs M	Yes, it did, Mrs Barker. Just a minute. Where's David?

Peter   What, Mr Mackintosh? I'll go and wake him.
Exit Peter upstairs.
Mrs M   I think I'll go and make some tea.
Exit Mrs M. through dining room door. There is general chat while she makes tea. After a while she enters, carrying a tray with tea cups on it. Peter rushes downstairs.
Peter   It's Mr Mackintosh. He's dead!
Mrs M. drops the cups and faints. Curtain.

In all fairness, I should say that this was a first attempt, undertaken completely independently, by a boy whose improvisation work was brilliant and who contributed most intelligently to any play-making exercise. He needed help and encouragement and went on to produce dialogue that was better paced and developed (see his second effort, quoted on p. 96).

The setting for the play quoted was the same throughout the four acts, but this was uncommon in apprentice playwriting efforts where there were frequently swift changes of action from one location to another, sometimes facilitated by the use of a narrator, but on other occasions making demands far beyond the possibilities of normal staging. A few lines in a banqueting hall are followed immediately by a scene in which the same characters are in the thick of a battle, in turn followed by an encounter on the battlements of a ruined castle, from which one character falls to drown, visibly, in the moat. The great majority of plays seen by children are television plays, and this shows in their writing.

There is, of course, nothing against the play in which action moves swiftly from one location to another – we produced many such plays, and so did Shakespeare – but it is essential to use quickly and simply established locations. A number of obligatory, elaborate, set-changes in a one-act play is not a practical proposition. Again, there is nothing intrinsically wrong with the 'television play' approach, provided the child does not want to present his play in conventional theatrical terms. Most children do, though. If they show interest, they can be helped to write increasingly viable plays, however maladroit their initial efforts may be. It is, of course, extremely important not to find their first efforts funny. They are generally only too well aware that their plays lack technical facility. What they need is the information on which to base progress, so it is equally important not to praise unthinkingly but to lead them to understand that play-writing, conventionally, requires much prior planning. Characters must be well considered and consistent, the plot must be well established, developed and sustained; the play should be capable of being presented in whatever medium the author has in mind, and possibly in others. As a general rule, children found it very difficult to fulfil these requirements in their individual attempts at writing plays.

In some English sets, teachers increasingly encouraged the children to experiment with telling a story in dialogue, supplemented by stage directions or narration. This hybrid form was often very successful. It did not, as a general rule, produce plays which could be presented visually, but often resulted in 'radio' scripts which could then be read or recorded by a group of children. Recording was generally more effective because sound effects could be used to give added realism and because listening to a disembodied tape made it easier to visualise the characters as the author intended them to be, rather than as children poring over a piece of paper. With this sort of script, swift transitions from one location to another did not present any particular difficulties. The dialogue thus produced would often have a naturalness and feeling for reality which did not always appear when a child settled down to 'write a play'. To the children, a play meant something essentially dramatic, and dramatic often came to mean essentially artificial. However, everyday situations could be conveyed realistically by this approach.

One class produced a series of scripts which simply narrated the events between waking in the morning and leaving the house. Before writing, they listened for a week, memorising and noting down the sort of conversations that took place. They were then given plenty of time to write their scripts: a very important point, this, for a hurried piece of work would almost inevitably fail to establish and develop itself satisfactorily. The scenes had a natural shape, with a beginning and end dictated by the requirements, and most of the class used an intensifying of the hurry and confusion to give the middle of their scenes forward impetus and climax. When the scripts were finished, they prepared readings of them for the rest of the class, sometimes gathered round the one book, sometimes – the most conscientious ones – working from cue scripts copied from the master copy. This approach was only variably effective, for children sometimes missed, or jumped, their cues, and sorting out the problems often led to a withdrawal of the audience's interest. Nevertheless the fact that the writers had listened to what had actually been said gave their dialogue authenticity; and that very authenticity drew smiles and laughs and caught the interest of the listeners far more readily than more artificial plays would have done. Certainly it was a more valuable exercise than the 'Let's explore this cave. Look! Diamonds!' sort of melodrama which children often seemed to feel was required in playwriting.

Even so, in the eyes of the children this sort of dialogue seemed to be an extension of standard composition work. It could be read aloud or taped, certainly, and it gave pleasure to the writers and the rest of the class, but it was not a 'real' play. Some children felt they wanted to go further, to write something which was readily identifiable as a play, for the idea held glamour for them. Dance Drama work often gave opportunities for shorter pieces of dialogue, linking the movement sections. In writing these the children did not come up against the problem of sustaining and developing work in order to produce a piece which would be satisfying to perform or to watch. In one Dance Drama, based on a Scandinavian legend, we were grateful for this piece of dialogue, offered by the first year boy whose work I have already quoted, for it established one character for us and helped to outline the situation, both of which had been causing us difficulty. The way he tackled it was left entirely up to him; all we had asked for was some dialogue to introduce the name of the character. Working on such a short piece, the boy was able to give fuller consideration to the effect of his dialogue, even to the deliberate repeating of 'here, there, everywhere', which linked the character with the supernatural elements. He was also able to choose his performers and produce the scene. After all, a play is written to be performed, and a playwright needs to hear his work given reality by actors if he is to evaluate it.

The acting area is empty as the farmer and the passer-by enter from opposite directions. As they pass the farmer speaks.

Farmer   'Ere! I wonder if you could help me. You see I want these posters put up around the village. I'll pay you for it. (*He hands him a wad of posters.*)

Passer-by   Yeh sure! 'Ere, what's this say? 'Wanted a shepherd.' A shepherd!

Farmer   What's the matter?

Passer-by   Well, it's going a bit far, isn't it? I mean putting posters up just for a shepherd – well it's just stupid.

Farmer   Well I have to do that. I'm still hoping to find someone with enough courage to stay at my farm, so I have to advertise all round the village.

Passer-by   But why, what's wrong with your farm?

Farmer   Well, it's just that it's haunted.

Passer-by   Haunted!

Farmer   Yes, in the night I hear strange and eerie noises. The whole house shakes. It seems full of evil. Everywhere I turn I hear noises, knockings and tappings. They're here, there, everywhere. No shepherd stays in my house after one night, I can tell you.

Passer-by   Yes, I can see your problem and I think I can help you.

Farmer   You can! How?

Passer-by   Well, I've seen this man around. He seems out of work so I'm sure he'd be glad of a job.

Farmer   But no man would stay at my farm for long.

Passer-by	This man would. He's ugly, mind you, and that's putting it mildly.
Farmer	But won't he be afraid?
Passer-by	Him no, he's as fearless as he is grotesque – so you're all right there. Glam, his name is.
Farmer	Fine, when can I meet him?
Passer-by	Who can say? He's over here, he's over there – he's here, there, everywhere all at once. Don't worry, you'll meet him, and when you do, ask him to become your shepherd. Good-bye.
Farmer	Goodbye and thanks.

It seemed that a useful way of sustaining the development of a dramatic idea was to spread the work among a group of children. We tried this in various ways with the script of *The Sword* (see Impetus). As a class exercise, I found that, for me, the most fruitful approach was to take a theme which would lend itself to a picaresque treatment and then to link dialogue produced by children in the class to make one continuous play. Whereas a smaller group could have produced a tightly-knit play, a class, while it could achieve unanimity on characters and development of plot, would not normally work in the same, closely interacting way, and so I felt that a less unified story line would suit them better. With one first year group, I built on the story of *Everyman*. This was a theme I had used once before with success and I therefore felt reasonably confident about using it. I had also learned from my mistakes in my previous treatment of the idea. I did not introduce the story to them straight away, for I wanted to be sure that the idea would interest them. It would have been sad to have committed us all to a project which did not engage the enthusiasm of the children. If I had started by announcing that, come what may, we were going to write this play, I might well have found that I had embarked on an undertaking in which only I was interested, which would have been dispiriting both for them and for me. No doubt a play could have been produced that way, but it would have meant concentration on the end product to the exclusion of the educational process which should have led to it. So, I approached the idea obliquely with a general consideration of Miracle and Mystery plays, building on work which they had done in their History lessons. Their interest was engaged and some of the class did individual research on the subject which they presented to the rest of the class as a basis for discussion.

They were intrigued by the idea of characters representing abstract qualities; this was new to them. We discussed whether it really was, in essence, completely different from current practice. At first they felt it was, basing their belief more on the nomenclature than anything else. They felt that to call a character 'Strength' in a television series, for instance, would be too bald. Then I gave the names of some of the characters in Restoration and later plays and from this we moved to a consideration of names which seemed to carry particular connotations: Fritz, Spud, Albert, Flossie. Someone recalled characters in children's TV called 'Brains', 'Speedy' and the like. They started to think about television characters and reached the conclusion that, especially in the run-of-the-mill series, one personality could well be established simply on one basic characteristic, even though he might well not be named after it. They could recall instances also of abstract characters in some television programmes – one representing Fate, for example. This led us to talk of the character Death. Some children did not see how he could be represented in a modern context, but others disagreed, visualising him first rather as something out of a Hammer film, but then coming round to the view that he would in fact be more frightening if he were unobtrusive, nebulous even. I read them the opening of *Everyman*, which they found interesting but difficult to accept; to them the voice of God was essentially a private voice, not overheard by anyone else, even in a dramatic situation. They did not have the Victorian child's conditioning towards pictures of God and Death. They felt that the unexpectedness of Death was right. That, to them, was an essential characteristic. They started to draw modern parallels in which Death could appear

as a warning in some situation: as a traffic policeman, halting
a speeding car; as a reflection in a mirror; an unexpected guest
at a party. Or where a climber, off balance, puts out his hand
for support, but the hand which takes hold of his is Death's.
By now, they were keen to take this idea further, to interpret
the idea of the play in modern terms. We went on to talk over
which characters they would introduce and how they could be
presented. Death, they felt, must introduce himself first.

*A game of pontoon is in progress. A pool of light round the table,
where Everyman sits, with Fred and Richard. Money, cards on
the table; also glasses and a couple of beer bottles.*

Fred   Your turn. I'm sticking.

Everyman Pontoon!

Triumphantly, he lays down the cards and collects fifty pence.

Richard   (*Thoroughly disgusted*) That's the fifth game you've
won in a row.

Everyman again deals the cards, smiling.

Fred   (*Miserably*) Not much money left.

Richard   Well, what's doing?

Fred   I dunno . . . er, I'll take one. (*Everyman gives him
a card.*) I'll twist again. (*Everyman gives him
another card*) And again. (*With a satisfied smile*)
I'll stick.

Everyman Well, what about you then, Dick? Fred's got a
five-card trick.

Richard   I'm sticking,

Everyman (*Turns over his cards, triumphant*) Another Pontoon. Pay five cards only.

Richard   You're in luck this evening, Everyman. Not thinking of backing out now?

Fred   (*Picking up some money*) At last. Money's rolling in.

Everyman Excuse me, fellows, I've run out of drinks up here.
I'll have to go down to the cellar to get some more –
I'll be back in a moment.

*Everyman goes down the steps to another part of the acting area,
Dim light on him. The pool of light on the players also dims a*

99

*little. He strikes a match, then looks up in fear as he sees a vague
shape standing in the shadows, watching him.*

Everyman Who . . . are . . . you?

The light goes out, and he fumbles for another match.

Death   I am the unquestionable Death.

Everyman (*On a long breath*) H...e...l...l...o... Death.

Death   There's no need to be afraid, Everyman. I have
been sent to tell you that you have very little time
before you have to go on a long journey to death.

Everyman But I'm not ready yet. I'm too young, surely. Oh,
please don't make me go.

Death   I am sorry, Everyman. You must go.

Everyman But what about my job – we're at a very crucial
stage. Why take me? Why not take them?

Death   Their turn will come. Now, it is you who must make
the journey.

Everyman (*Desperately pleading*) Why me, why did you have
to pick me, when I have everything to live for. I
have my wife, my family, my work, everything.

Death   (*Softly and sympathetically*) I'm sorry. Truly I am,
but I cannot help you. My master has instructed
me, and I must obey him.

Eventually, however, he manages to persuade Death to allow
him to try and find others to accompany him on the journey.
Those who would be approached in our version were decided
after much discussion. There was Kindred, who was to be
represented by a selfish, complaining elderly aunt who was
always wishing herself dead, but who changes her mind when
approached by Everyman, deciding that life still has attrac-
tions for her, despite her ailments. There was Wealth, effusive,
egocentric, carelessly rich, at first attracted by the idea of the
long journey, but haughtily rejecting Everyman on hearing
the destination; Wisdom, an ageing and rather stock-type
scientist, who decides that 'the grave may be interesting, from
a scientific point of view, after all; it should be quite an experience to go to Death'; Strength, very proud of his virility, but

rather simple and given to boasting; and Good Looks, feckless, superficial and vain:

Good Looks   Hello . . . who is that marvellously strong young man?

Wisdom   Me? (*Wistfully*) I was handsome in my day.

Looks   (*Smothering herself with cream*) Not you, you silly old man. (*Pointing to Strength*) Him.

Strength   (*With mock modesty*) Me? Oh, well, I suppose I do happen to have superhuman strength.

Everyman   (*To Wisdom*) I wonder if she will come?

Looks   (*Gazing at herself in the mirror*) What are you muttering about? My beauty . . . you don't have to tell me, I know already. *Everyone* talks about my beauty.

Everyman   No...o...o. You see, I'm afraid I have to go on a journey,

Looks   What's the matter with going on a journey? (*With an affected drawl*) You meeeet people.

Everyman   It's not that sort of journey. This is a journey to death.

Looks   O...o...h! So soon! Well Wisdom and Strength are there with you; why don't you ask them if they will accompany you?

Everyman   I have, and they are coming. Will you come, too?

Looks   Well, all right, but only for a way. If we go beyond a certain point of pleasure in life, I will lose all my good looks.

Good Deeds, who has been ailing, is revived by Everyman's prayers. This was the most nebulous of all the characters. The children were anxious to avoid a pious, priggish character, but this seemed to produce a rather hearty do-gooding type. Eventually, Good Deeds came out very nondescript. The only thing the children were positive about was that it should be a female character. The only other person that the class were keen to include was Five Wits, a character with considerably heightened perception. They felt that to include more could make the play confusing, especially as we decided to divide it up into sections in order to make it easier for individual contributions to be made to the group work. We decided on nine sections in all; in the first seven Everyman meets Death and then, one after another, approaches Kindred, Wealth, Wisdom, Strength, Good Looks and Five Wits. In the last two, Good Deeds is revived and joins the journeying group; then, near to the grave, they all leave him, except Good Deeds, who stays with him till the last.

They were given plenty of time in class and at home to work on the script. We tackled it in two parts: Sections One to Six first, then Sections Seven and Eight. Each person could decide which section he wanted to write for. I felt it was better to allow this freedom of choice rather than take it section by section with compulsory contributions to each from all the children, for I felt this could lead to a diminution in interest. I could have ensured that sufficient dialogue was produced for each section by allocating certain children to write dialogue for specific parts of the play; but I felt it was more important for them to write on whichever parts particularly caught their interest, even if that meant that one part of the play might be represented only thinly, or not at all, when we came to collect the dialogue together. If that happened, then more groundwork would be required on that portion, and I could again ask for contributions, As it happened, this was not necessary, for each episode had been included after enthusiastic advocacy, and the advocates now set about translating their enthusiasm into dialogue.

Once this was written, they gathered in groups to read it, not at first to the class, but for the writers to hear what it sounded like. They found this useful, for the ultimate test of dialogue is how it performs, and the authors were then able to amend their work if it did not come over as they had intended it. The comments of the rest of the group were helpful, too. When they were all reasonably satisfied, the scenes were read to the rest of the class for discussion and comment. The children were quick to draw a distinction between good dialogue and good performance of a less worthy script. Generally, one script emerged in each section as the fullest or most effective treatment of it, but others also contained ideas or pieces of dialogue worth preserving. The class talked for some time about the possibility of combining strengths to produce corporate scripts. It became apparent that full class discussion, though valuable, was nevertheless too cumbersome a method by which to arrive at a final script. So they elected a committee to take off all the contributions and, bearing in mind the comments and ideas raised in the class discussions, to produce a full script of the first part.

Each member of the committee started by specialising on one section, reading through the various contributions, and marking each script with his own notes and comments. Then they came together and discussed the play scene by scene, with the person responsible for each section performing the wearying task of copying out the agreed final version. This version was then presented to the class while the committee defended any queried decisions: one episode, though highly effective, was not in keeping with the character as the class had envisaged him and as he appeared in the rest of the play; some lines which had been added by the committee had been necessary to ease the transition from one section to another, and so on. Some further agreed amendments were made, and that part of the script was finished.

The second part contained only two sections, but it seemed to me that they were much less well-defined than those in the first part. I asked the children to approach these sections in any way they liked, and deliberately avoided drawing up the rather rigid outlines which we had used in the first part. As a result of this, and also perhaps because their enthusiasm was diminishing, a number of contributions were rather perfunctory. We had given a lot of thought and concentration to the first sections, and when we had gone through all the processes and produced a final script, a number of the children felt that really that was the end of the writing part of the exercise and didn't feel the same enthusiasm for the continuation.

103

I could have managed this rather better, but as it happened, the extra freedom enabled others to introduce interesting individual ideas. One child was engrossed by the thought of Five Wits' loss of faculties, realising that this was a reflection of Everyman's condition and so presenting it in human terms:

Everyman (*In despair*) I cannot cope with this life any longer. I want to die now.

Deeds You mustn't talk like that.

Wits (*Suddenly*) I . . . can't feel the buttons on my coat.

His fingers grope and feel in great despair.

Wits Where is . . . Strength . . . and . . . Wisdom . . . and Everyman . . . where are you?

He outstretches his hands and feels the air.

Everyman Here, Five Wits, here.

Wits Where . . . I cannot feel you . . . or see . . . you.

Strength (*With compassion*) Alas! You are gradually dwindling away, poor fellow, poor Five Wits.

Wisdom Come come, now. You are jumping to conclusions; don't try to imagine Five Wits is at his end.

Wits (*Stumbling*) Good Deeds, help me, help me back. I cannot see, I am blind. Oh God, I'm losing all my senses, I cannot feel or see any more.

Everyman Here, drink this, Five Wits.

Wits (*Taking a sip*) There's no taste to this wine . . . or is it me? And all that I can smell is an awful, breath-catching aroma. Oh, help me back, please, even if it's only for a short way.

He stretches out his hands and stumbles out of sight.

Another child introduced two Evils, one, the Evil of Everyman's youth, the other, of his manhood. Though the treatment of the idea was somewhat naïve, nevertheless the idea itself caught the interest of the other children and so it was included. Another child (who certainly never read *Our Town*) developed the idea that Everyman should find himself watching the mourners at his own funeral.

The committee's job in putting together the second part was

relatively easy, for it was generally agreed that about half a
dozen of the contributions contained the bulk of worthwhile
ideas and lines, although others, even though not of the same
overall standard, could nevertheless contribute a striking line
or two. They felt that one or two moments in the play needed
strengthening, and asked the class for poems or prayers to pre-
cede the revival of Good Deeds and to end the play. Not all the
children contributed these, only those who were particularly
interested. When two of the prayers and one of the poems had
been chosen the final script was ready. They cast it and performed it in an informal festival. It ran for about the length of
a conventional one-act play, though we wished that we had had
the time to have developed it with movement and crowd work
into a half an evening's programme, which we could well have
done. A very mixed audience, from younger brothers and sisters
to visiting dignitaries, received it well. The cast would have
rather liked to repeat it, but I felt that this was not a good idea.
As a project, it had completeness; the idea had caught their
interest, had been developed in a way individual to them, had
reached a final stage and been shared with an interested
audience.

I could have done one more thing, though: given each child
a copy of the script; but I didn't think about it at the time,
though I did give copies of later plays to children who had
made them. I used this approach of shared writing of plays
with a number of different classes, sometimes taking a very
loose framework, sometimes dividing the class into groups,
each producing a section of a previously discussed and plotted
play. I did not manage to produce any solo playwrights by this
means, but a lot of children were actively involved in the process of writing a play. I would very much have liked to have
been involved in the staging of the world première of an original
play by, perhaps, one of our sixth formers, but I found that,
while they readily produced shorter pieces of dialogue and
scenes for inclusion in group projects, no one came up with
a full play. Perhaps it was too much to expect, or perhaps the
group method of writing a script was not the best preparation

Drama casebook

for writing complete plays. Anyway, the involvement of larger
numbers of children in the playwriting process was perhaps
more valuable. Certainly, if the Impetus work had been able to
develop as I had hoped it would, sooner or later someone would
have arrived with a script for production, and certainly someone would have put it on, for the only real way for a playwright
to begin his work is to see it in production. As it was, the sixth
form English work became increasingly an extension of 'A'
level, which was encouraging for Shakespeare, but not for
young authors.

Chapter 6

Dance Drama

Each evening after school, one major activity had priority, and Friday was Drama Club evening. The club was run in the gym for about an hour and a quarter, though the members would certainly have preferred a longer time. I took the sessions with the assistance of another member of the Drama staff, and then as time went on she took the sessions with my help. We had a limited number of children in the club. In the early days of the school, we had groups of as many as two hundred but we found this led to difficulties of organisation – for instance, in a relaxation exercise, it became impossible for them all to find sufficient space in which to lie down without bumping against other people. We found also that the large numbers inhibited the organic growth of ideas, and the sessions tended to develop into periods when the children followed our instructions and didn't really have the chance to develop their own interpretations. The results were effective enough but were, I felt, too imposed. We found that, for us, the viable number was between forty and sixty. This meant, in practice, that first and second year children had to work separately, the first year using a lunch-time (which was limiting) until about half-way through the Summer term, when they took over the Friday evening sessions after the second year children had given performances of their Dance Drama. It also meant a certain amount of selection, which is something I try to avoid wherever possible. However, we were able to ensure a representative selection, and we found that we could safely start with greater numbers than we really wanted because there were always some who dropped out for one reason or another. We kept a waiting list, and from this we kept up the numbers to a practicable level, trying to keep the group balanced and fully representative – not all of them extravert or highly sensitive or particularly agile or very intelligent or conformist, for instance. We took care, also, to keep a balance between the numbers of boys and girls.

With each new group, we started generally, not developing a specific theme, but hoping that one would develop in time. We found that a loose framework was more fruitful for us. I know that there have been many instances of successful Dance Dramas coming from the treatment of a specific story, but we never seemed to be able to work well that way; the story tended to be inhibiting. One Dance Drama which we based on a Scandinavian folk tale proved to be completely bewildering to the audiences. We found also that, for us, following too precisely any particular piece of music also tended to be too restrictive; although, again, I know of a number of instances when, for instance, a tone poem had been most successfully interpreted in dance. I think it was really a question of the way that we worked and the empirical manner in which our Dance Drama tended to come about. In the following accounts of three Dance Dramas, I will try to show how they originated and developed into performances.

Dance Drama. *Space*

This piece had its origin in one particular exercise. We had been experimenting with taking one short scene at three speeds: standard, fast and slow, rather as if a film had first been projected at normal speed, then speeded up, then slowed down, with the speech also altered in speed and pitch, which added to the fun of the activity. Very soon, a number of the groups found that it was difficult to manage falls at slow speed. For instance, one member of a group, starting a dignified exit after an argument, had to trip and fall, losing his dignity. When we came to see each other's work – for we found that analysis of the movement and critical appraisal by others was always useful – we saw that some groups had overcome their problem (or avoided it) by judicious choice of the type of fall. Some of the falls, for instance, could be performed in short sequences: someone who has been shot can sag, clasp his stomach, sink to his knees, slowly collapse, unrolling the spine, and so avoid at any time having a distance to fall. Another way was for the faller to use support – a wall, another person standing by – to sustain him so that his fall could be as slow as he wished. Someone who had just been poisoned could fall forward, catching the shoulder of the poisoner and slowly dragging his hands down the body of the other, rolling clear when he reached the floor. But the dignified person tripping over a mat could not use such a device and so the criticism of his fall was that it lacked smoothness and flow. It was too obviously a fairly quick and jerky move through a series of positions, given some semblance of slowness by a pause at these positions, but discontinuous and not really conveying the effect.

We discussed this for a while and decided that this slow movement needed to be very carefully planned and practised to avoid jerkiness or sudden changes in balance. The scientific thought in terms of centres of gravity and the intuitive started to try it out. Soon, everyone was working on this, with something like the effect of under-water movement: slow, smooth, flowing. They tried all sorts of variations: rolling over, falling, or moving up from a prone position by swinging their legs up and supporting themselves on their shoulders and completing what was, in effect, a backward roll. Some worked singly, some in pairs, some in groups. Holst's 'Uranus' was on the record player, so we used that. The whole effect was very beautiful, with the fluent, slow movements enhanced by the music.

This took place at about the time of the first Space Walk, and the similarities were immediately obvious. This became the beginning of our Dance Drama *Space* and we felt encouraged to think of other ways in which to use various exercises from our club sessions in telling our story. The final work was made up of such exercises, but used to carry the story, to convey feelings and ultimately to make a comment on civilisation.

1. THE LAUNCHING

To light-hearted music – the Walton *Johannesburg Festival Overture* – a festive crowd arrives for the official launching of the rocket. Some picnic, some watch sideshows, some play games, some simply relax in the sun. The two astronauts go through and attract considerable interest. The actual launching is rather like the opening of a fête: an elderly gentleman, accompanied by a mixed group of officials and ladies in hats, presses the button and after three unsuccessful attempts, the rocket unexpectedly goes off when everyone has lost interest (the rocket is not seen; all this is conveyed in the crowd's reactions.)

This sequence grew from the crowd work done in the Club sessions. Sometimes we did a beach scene, sometimes a market, sometimes a fair, and so on. The children became used to creating characters to people these situations, reacting in character to whatever happened in loosely structured scenes. The episode of the delayed launching derived from an exercise in which groups were supposedly watching something; the rest of us watched them and, from their actions and reactions, tried to re-create what they were seeing. One group had pretended to be saboteurs, peering through the darkness as one of them pressed the button to activate an explosive charge. After a number of failures, they gave up in disgust and turned away, whereupon the force of the explosion knocked them over. All this, in mime, was neat and clear, so we felt it would be amusing to adapt the idea for the whole group to use in the Dance Drama.

2. THE WALK IN SPACE (TO 'URANUS')

This was the one section in the completed Dance Drama which was not done by the entire group. It seemed logical to do it this way as it made the story clearer. The two astronauts were the only people in complete costume, which distinguished them from the other characters, who wore their usual Drama Club outfit – jeans, slacks, tee shirts, PE kit, that sort of thing.

110

3. MEETING THE INHABITANTS

The aimless, grey creatures of the planet wander on. No music for this; they make their own sounds, humming in different pitches, whistling very softly, making an extended 'shh' sound. As the astronauts enter, the sound intensifies then stops abruptly. The inhabitants move towards the intruders, at first hesitating, then menacing. The threatened astronauts switch on powerful torches; menace ends; the inhabitants submit.

This scene grew from the following sources: conversation carried on without the use of real words, by using sounds or gibberish noises; group work in concentrating on an object which inspires fear (originally, each group decided the nature of the object and the outcome for themselves); different kinds of walk – in this instance, lethargic, purposeless movement; pair work in which one threatens the other but is finally over-come, without physical force.

4. THE INHABITANTS AWAKE TO HAPPINESS

To the tenth movement from the *Miracle in the Gorbals* Suite, by Bliss. All the inhabitants are lying asleep. Gradually, as the music starts, life starts to come into their hands, then arms, their head, then the whole body. The music becomes lighter and more rhythmic. It draws them up and they leap and dance and play.

This was a standard exercise for beginning the actual sessions. Generally while the people were getting changed and gathering in the gym, improvised games were played – versions of basket-ball, British Bulldog, tag, or other games in pairs or small groups. So when the session began, everyone started flat on the floor, completely relaxed. Then it became the custom to play some music and for the inert bodies to come to life gradually in response to this. The music varied but always – because of its function – started gently. Sometimes it remained gentle – like Copland's *Our Town* music or the second and third *Rodeo* dances, or Vaughan Williams' Pastoral Symphony or his *Lark Ascending*. Sometimes, it became more animated, like the first movement of Dvořák's Eighth Symphony or Job's Dream from

Vaughan Williams' *Job* which starts by representing Job's quiet sleep and then becomes more menacing as Satan fills his dreams with visions of plague, war and destruction. Thus, the children had become used to listening to the music and responding to it.

5. THE CONTROLS

The astronauts arrange for messages from earth to reach the minds of some of the inhabitants and their actions are controlled from earth. Using the 9th of Britten's 'Frank Bridge' Variations, another exercise in coming to life from relaxation.

6. THE CONTROLS DOMINATE THE REST

No music; but clapping, stamping, percussive sounds, humming, sharp cries. One of the problems which arises in Drama work is that some groups of boys tend to spend a great deal of their time in scuffles and downright scrimmages which, though obviously enjoyable to the participants, can be difficult to justify educationally. Some teachers simply ban fights; others limit them: 'Right, that's enough fighting – get on with the play.' I found that my own most useful approach was to require that any fights should be well managed and should look effective, which spontaneous or disorganised fights often don't, but not be dangerous, as those fights sometimes can be. In any production, players involved in a fight would spend a long time working it out, stage by stage in the gym. I also found it useful to ask groups to work out scenes of violence without any physical contact. This is difficult, requiring painstaking preparation, but it generally conveys far more impression of conflict than a bit of rolling round or scuffling. It was on this work that this sequence was based: about half a dozen groups, each performing separately, for each group needed the full space available. Some groups used the idea of slow, cumulative menace with a heavy stamping rhythm but most used at least some fast, wide running or leaping, and it would have been inhibiting for even two such groups to have been working at the same time. When the individual sequences were finished, the whole group, using 'Job's Dream', worked together in a scene in which the stronger few dominated the rest, controlling them like puppets. This grew from paired work, at first an extension of the idea of drawing people up as if they were puppets on strings – one arm, one leg, both arms, whole body – then cutting the strings so that the puppet falls lifeless. This idea was then extended to the control of a partner over a greater distance with increasingly subtle gestures and signals.

7. THE INHABITANTS ARE SET TO WORK

The children much enjoyed being machines, sometimes singly but more often in groups, together making a more complex machine. About six of them would work as a unit; perhaps two standing apart, hands joined, arms pumping as pistons; others perhaps lifting or swinging or rotating another person; others maybe bobbing up and down, or moving mechanically between one part of the machine and the other, or rolling backwards and forwards. All the parts interacting, and all making their own mechanical sounds. No music to this piece, either: the sounds were sufficient in themselves.

8. JOY TURNS TO HORROR

To more music from *Miracle in the Gorbals*, the joy at finishing work turns to horror as plague strikes down the inhabitants. From another exercise, on falls. The children had experimented with many kinds of fall – a slow crumpling; leaping for a ball and collapsing at the height of the jump; in the middle of an argument, suddenly falling; doing some simple mechanical action; swinging a partner round; dancing – an infinite variety.

9. THE REMAINING INHABITANTS DESTROY THE ASTRONAUTS AND RETURN TO THEIR FORMER GREYNESS

This section was based on the exercises in sections 3 and 6. The additional source was work on carrying bodies. Particularly in an arena production, where the audience can be very conscious of lately dead characters scurrying off, one has to decide how to get rid of the bodies. In the Dance Drama, as each section closed, the lights faded and the characters simply moved off, but in a play – and at this climatic point of the Dance Drama – something else was necessary. The Shakespearean precedent is a valuable one, but it must be done well: a Hamlet whose head is struck heavily on an archway, a Lear who slowly sags out of the hold of his staggering bearers, cannot be said to have gained dignity in death. The children had learned that care and preparation are necessary if the person is to be lifted, carried and deposited to good effect. In this scene, to the end of the 'Gorbals' music, the dead astronauts were lifted high, heads hanging back downwards, then placed on steps, still with the heads lolling back, as the grey people drifted into immobility, It was very moving, yet it had grown from the weekly exercises.

The story itself assisted, of course. A fortunate development also helped. A number of the children had talked over the ideas of the work with their contemporaries, and the themes of the Dance Drama were mentioned fairly frequently in English lessons. Soon, children in the group, and others who were interested but not directly involved, were wanting to use the ideas as a focus and stimulus for writing, especially for writing poetry. The Head of English herself became very interested and discussed the possibility of a wider use of the Dance Drama as a stimulus for writing. We found that it was possible to take groups of four classes at a time to the gym, with their teachers, to explain the context of the extract they were going to see, to let the Drama Club go through the piece for them and then to break up again into smaller groups for discussing and writing. Some of the poems and dialogue thus produced were used for linking episodes and as commentary on them. The dialogue was between people on earth – scientists, lecturers, ordinary people in pubs and so on – and prepared the way for each section of the movement work. These sections were produced and performed by the writers and their friends. The poems were spoken from steps on either side of the working area, by the writer if he or she wished it, or by other volunteers, speaking the poems individually or in groups. Sometimes, as in 'The Walk in Space', the poems would accompany the action; sometimes they would be interjected; generally the action ended and the poem followed. This idea came rather late in the development of this Dance Drama because at first it had not occurred to me what an excellent focus such a project could make for related work in other subjects. However, the children enjoyed the writing and produced some thoughtful poems.

Astronaut in Space

I glide around,
Nothing moves but me.
Me, in this vast wilderness of black,
The only thing that moves through time.

Planets move, they do not know it.
Meteors move, they do not know it.
Only I know what it is like
Moving, moving through the huge wilderness of
time.

The Strangers

Through the grey and aimless night,
Two strangers came with torches bright
That lit the landscape here and there
Then moved along, like restless air.

We, grey and lifeless, dead and loath,
Drifted up to touch their clothes,
Caught the disease and now we lie
Blind and groping while they pass by.

The Machine: a Man

(This poem was spoken by two people, on opposite sides of the
working area: one spoke positively, the other replied in a
mechanical voice)

> You will not be able to do anything not instructed.
> You show no sorrow to be without a mind?
>
> What is sorrow? I have no mind, no soul, no will.
> I show happiness only if I am instructed, I die when
>   I am told to.
> You see, the core of me has been gouged out
> If the machine breaks down, I break down
> I am dead, my soul is gone.
>
> Do you not want to be a man again?
>
> I cannot want unless I am told to want.
> You see it is not me speaking, it is the machine . . .
> the machine . . . the machine . . . the machine . . .

A number of children did related paintings, too, so we
mounted an exhibition of these, with copies of many of the
poems, for the audience to wander round after the performance.
I use the word 'performance', but it is not really appropriate.
We sat the visitors around the working area, transferred from
the gym to a hall for practical reasons. Numbers were necessarily
limited and the visitors – parents, staff colleagues, groups from
Colleges of Education and so on – were invited; it was not a
public performance. The aim was to re-create the atmosphere of
a usual working session as far as this was possible. At the beginning, the children filtered into the working area as they were
ready, starting their games and warming-up work. Then we
went through some of the work of a usual Club evening. Finally,
we did what we called 'The Thing', which lasted about an
hour and a quarter.

    I wonder if this attempt to re-create the regular situation
was not perhaps more artificial than presenting a straight-

forward performance; rather like those evenings in historical places where period costume is worn, period music is played and period food eaten by unalterably contemporary people, all trying to convince everyone that this is what the real thing must have been like. Nevertheless, I used the same pattern for all my subsequent Dance Drama because I felt that it did at least produce a situation in which experience and work could be shared rather than displayed. Certainly, the audiences found the experience worthwhile. I talked to numbers of those who came and watched the Dance Drama *Space*. All had been moved; some had been excited, some, disturbed, by the intensity of the work. They were impressed by the concentration, too. Paradoxically, I have always found that one of the great advantages of arena work to be that the children are generally less aware of the audience, though they may be so near to it as to come, sometimes, into physical contact. But it is not sitting in one slab, dictating the direction of the performance, producing a massed, corporate response; it is diffused, more individual, somehow more intimate. In the plague scene when one body collapsed and 'died' on to the feet of some members of the audience, they were far more concerned than the body who remained inert and unaware of them until the end of the scene, when she popped up and moved away still apparently unaware of them as they shifted about trying to clear themselves of the pins and needles.

Inevitably, however, some element of The Show must be there. The really interesting part of the work is in the actual Club sessions when ideas suddenly materialise and the whole group is enthused and interacts, expanding and developing the first ideas. For instance: once, when we were working towards the Dance Drama *Ritual*, some boys who had formed a group with guitars and percussion had offered to compose a song for us. They came to the gym one Friday evening and played it to us, with another folk song. The members of the Club were relaxing after an active period and as the group started the music, thrumming guitars and singing their folk melodies, gradually everyone started to respond, growing upwards from their prone positions as if towards light. It was tremendously moving, and essentially unrepeatable. We didn't work on it any more, but we used it to end the Dance Drama towards which we were working at that time. In this context, it was still extremely moving and it affected the audience deeply. But it was still not quite the same – it was not the original moment of creation, but a reproduction of it. We did the work twice, then we were finished with it which was fortunate because the essential quality would not have survived repeated performances. I am not saying that the scene could not have been performed over and over again, producing its effect, moving its audience; but the quality would have been different, the inspiration would have to be replaced by technique. That is not necessarily better or worse, but it is different. The Club sessions were really an opportunity for group creative work; inevitably, there was a wish to show, or share, or communicate, the results – from myself as well as from the children. The performances served as a focus, a discipline – a stimulus, too.

As I saw it, a Dance Drama had, for us, to serve a different purpose from that of a production. This was an attempt to draw together work in progress for sharing with a group of interested people. Inevitably, the final shape was not completely decided by the children; we staff had necessarily selected and shaped material, if only by our encouragement of certain aspects of the work, and the overall pattern tended to be finalised by us. The children contributed the ideas, the enthusiasm, the commitment; the staff had to encourage these qualities to coalesce into something which had unity and could be communicated. It was not always easy to reflect the children's viewpoint, especially if we were strongly committed to a viewpoint of our own. It was easy to convince ourselves on occasions that this was what the children really meant, or would have meant if they had considered things more deeply. It was also easy to pre-decide a direction, and to inhibit the development of an idea that didn't really fit in with a preconceived pattern, but which could have been better, perhaps, when it had grown. Later, older groups of children worked together without staff involvement to produce their own Dance Drama; that they were able and keen to do so was probably the fairest indication of their full involvement in, and understanding of, the process by which a Dance Drama could be evolved. They were not just repetitions of the earlier pattern though: at one point, the influence of *West Side Story* predominated over all others; on another occasion, one fairly small group worked out a Dance Drama which had no music or sound at all, just movement. It was explicit and impressive. The movement work carried over, too, into their own productions. One sixth former evolved her own notation for movement, which worked very well for her and for those who worked with her.

The early Dance Dramas tended to be isolated from the academic work of the school, partly because they derived from a club activity, not a lesson, but also partly because there was in the early days some feeling that Drama was a 'fringe' activity which, though it could fruitfully be used to give another dimension to a more established subject, had not the stature necessary to sustain a central role in a project. Fortunately, staff responded with increasing enthusiasm and interest as the possibilities of related work became evident. In the programme of a later Dance Drama, *Ritual*, I wrote:

'This term, we have again used our Dance Drama activities as the focus for much other work. The Club itself meets after school on Friday evenings, from four o'clock until they can be persuaded to leave. This year, we have given the First Years a separate time because of pressure of numbers, so the Friday group consists only of Second Years, but with some visiting Third Years. It is difficult, on reflection, to say how the ideas first suggest themselves: often, a movement exercise will develop a dramatic impulse, and that is how the Nightmare sequence grew; sometimes, an external stimulus starts a train of thought – a teacher brought some Voodoo masks to school and this stimulated a lot of ideas, particularly the 'mask' sequence. Music, too provided a stimulus – the whole of the last section, when good finally triumphs, grew from two songs, one original, one the Folk Song, "Come with me now".

'The work is never finally set, and it cannot be emphasised strongly enough that this evening's work session is not in any respect a "show". It is simply an attempt to gather together the various aspects of work which have, during the term, grown from the Dance Drama sessions. For instance, we have sometimes gathered groups of children – a hundred to a hundred and fifty at a time – to see some of the ideas being worked out. They then went back to their classrooms, discussed, argued, wrote. Others made masks, others produced music and so on.

'What this evening attempts to be is a substitute – admittedly a very thin one – for a wander round the school when the work was actually in progress. That way, one would have seen the work growing and developing. Such a wander could well have started in the Gym, where children were watching members of the Club working, say on the Bonfire sequence; then, with them, back to their English lessons to hear the animated and often very perceptive discussion and to see how the poems grew from this; then to come to one of the Art rooms where an acrid smell and a shower of polystyrene chippings would indicate that masks were being designed and made in that particular medium; through another Art room with some children painting pictures inspired by the Mask sequence and others working on the black and white designs some of which, as screen prints, have been used as covers for programmes and magazines; next, an Art room full of children sticking coloured Cinamoid on to glass (and on to themselves) – making the slides which we back-projected on to the screen at various points in the Dance Drama. Next, odd percussive noises might draw you to the Music room to see a class recording music, using not only the more conventional percussion instruments but also home-made ones of much ingenuity. In another room, perhaps, the sound of guitars, and songs being rehearsed. Next, workshops: metal masks being designed and produced. Afterwards, in the hall, a group of boys working on the switchboard, going through their own lighting plot for this evening.

'As the work has grown, we have tried to gather it together, not selecting "the best", but trying to convey a little of the excitement of the creative work.'

Dance Drama *Ritual*

The work was developing and widening in scope. A proportion of the final Thing came, again, from the exercises. But the initial idea had come from the Voodoo masks lent by a teacher who was using them in a Humanities study of primitive man. We had put them on the gym floor and the children walked round them, looking at them, afraid to go near them (rather as in the exercise which originated Section II of *Space*). Then one girl moved forward; touched a mask; slid her hands over its surface; took hold of it, examining it, her fingers exploring its smoothness. She lifted it, held it for a moment, then deliberately put it on. Stillness. Then the body began to move in increasing frenzy. The mask had taken control of the wearer. This is how it was described by someone who had watched the action:

> Feeling the mask's empty sinister eyes,
> Grinning mouth, sinister hair,
> Feeling of evil and darkness,
> Empty, dark, meaningless nothingness –
> Until you put it on and then you become something –
> Something of hate and blind fury –
> Fury, to do pain to someone,
> Under the control of the mask.
> The empty eyes have become evil,
> The grinning mouth has become yours.
> The sinister hair has become chains
> To lock you in the mask.
> It is your face now.
> You have allowed it take over your body.
> You now have to accept it.

Once the idea of ritual and witchcraft had occurred to us, it was surprising how it shaped the work and gave it a particular ambience. In one Club session, our crowd scene was based on

bonfire night – it was about the time of November 5th and it is
often fruitful to use seasonal or topical events as a starting
point for such scenes. The children were gathering around the
bonfire, lighting fireworks and enjoying themselves, when the
boy who was the Guy began to move. In other circumstances,
no doubt, the scene would have developed in fun; the Guy would
have perhaps turned out to be a human who had fallen asleep
on the heap of wood. But this time, the response was different.
The playing children slowly stopped their activities. First,
disbelief, then terror came and they ran, screaming. Later,
the scene developed so that the children who had been the
flames in the bonfire also emerged, as witches, and gathered
round the Guy:

The fire seemed to blow up.
    As petrol fumes clouded the air
The mushroom cloud spread-eagled above
    All the joystricken children screaming with enjoyment.
In the shrill cries several bangs added to the assorted
                                           pleasure;
    Immediately extra-loud screams penetrated the bangs,
Stars followed red-coloured streaks.
    The night air was warm with excitement.

. . . It moved, it actually moved!
But this was the distortion of the blinding heat,
    It went unnoticed.
But eventually they noticed, as the flaming, soulless
                                    travesty of humanity
Rose from its throne with the crackle of dry straw from its
                                                    innards.
        The children had to stop then.
The rising figure made an avalanche of the wood
    As it sauntered down from the mound of planks.
Ear-piercing screams came from the children, their faces
                            illuminated, disbelieving.
It seemed to float down the burning mass, and then edged
                                                its way

Through the flames and into the night;
    It hesitated as if it was too cold.
The panic-striken children were running wildly away from
                                  the bonfire,
    Clasping, unconsciously, unused fireworks,
The flame-light flickering on their backs, and the soles of
                           shoes' quickening pace.
    Hidden figures, witches, arose from the eerie crackle of the
                                    flames.
The inhuman guy floundered back to his position,
    And the witches pranced round the flaming heap as if
                           worshipping him.

Again, the exercises mentioned in *Space* developed a particular emphasis now. We again used the idea of puppets, but the developments were sinister; although the children of one group did not know the story of *Petrushka*, they produced a scene which bore definite similarities.

          Like puppets
          The humans hang,
          Limp, lifeless
             Hung on strings.

          Strings,
             Unable to control their own movements
          Without a mind that thinks,
             Human puppets.

          Puppets,
             Slow moving,
          Jerky movements not smooth,
             Blank expressions on their faces.

In this version of the 'control' work, one person on the far side of the area mimed the sticking of pins into a wax doll; her distant partner responded, her reactions controlled by the subtle movements of the other.

> They came, they came, the pins came,
> Pins aimed at me,
> Pins, like daggers, aimed for my body,
> Piercing my skin,
> Letting the blood leak out of me.

Other groups 'harmed' their victim with the slightest of movements or sounds. The paired mirror work, too, developed in response to this theme of the supernatural. In this work, one person is the miror of the other, generally starting unadventurously with shaving or cleaning the teeth but often developing into far-ranging and ambitious movement work. It has to be done slowly at first, and the children have to realise that it is a joint exercise and not a competition. One evening, in their mirror work, one pair decided to change faces. This was an arresting idea, and it developed into this scene: each person gets up in the morning, yawning, not really awake, blankly following his usual routine. But when he looks in the mirror, the face he sees stares blankly back at him. It is not his. In panic, he moves into the street, where everyone else is desperately searching, too. Suddenly, he recognises a face. It is his own, but on another person. The other person comes towards him; very carefully, each peels off the other's face and replaces his own with it.

> The faces of the passers by
> Are full of worry; so am I.
> Who am I with the different face?
> Why was my other one so replaced?
>
> I walk along in quiet despair,
> Perhaps I'll find myself somewhere.
> A gasp beside me I hear,
> I look to see who it is there.
>
> A boy of my height, my hair,
> With my face, too, is standing there!
> We both, with one accord
> Stretched out hands and pulled.

Our fingers groped and peeled the skin,
The faces came off paper thin.
We smoothed them on again.
Surprised to feel no pain.

For one English group, consideration of witches led to *Macbeth*, and a couple of groups of girls worked on the three witches' scenes, which we included in the final Thing. Then others parodied the incantations:

Round and round the shop we go
Then in our baskets these we throw:

Murdered shrimps in handy tins,
Herrings sliced without their fins;
Leg of lamb, dripping with blood,
To make our evening meal so good;
Lobsters still with groping claws,
Kit-E-Kat for pussy's paws;
Aubergines, radish, burning hot;
Devilled ham and raw shallot.

Grumble, grumble, moan and mumble
Queueing, queueing, what a jumble!

Blood-red oranges, mottled deep;
Liver of sheep and tongue of pig;
(Our basket's store is getting big)
Liver of pig and tongue of sheep;
In the deep freeze take a peep.

Grumble, grumble, moan and mumble,
Queueing, queueing, what a jumble!

Shopkeeper cries, ''Tis time! 'Tis time!'
Green Shield Stamps I'll put in purse,
Of this day out, I'm none the worse.

Grumble, grumble, moan and mumble,
Queueing, queueing, what a jumble!

This led us to consider our own civilisation in terms of rituals and we followed the speaking of that poem with a formalised representation of a Supermarket in the final evening's performances, for which we now saw a pattern developing. The first part of the final Thing consisted of a series of episodes on ritual and the supernatural, loosely linked together as facets of a nightmare – the ritual harmings, the face exchanging, the bonfire and so on; the second part was cast as a commentary by people of the future on our own civilisation, considered rather as we ourselves view extinct primitive civilisations as strange, sometimes difficult to understand, with fragmentary evidence sometimes interpreted by surmise:

'We have a few relics from this era. This is one. We believe that this piece of plastic adorned with bristles dates back to the twentieth century. The people used to have one each, kept in a sacred place called the bathroom, and it was used to worship a substance called water. Water was one of their Gods. They used to put this instrument in their mouths and then put it under water, believing that the sounds they made with their mouths would be transferred to the water.

'Very strange habits they had in those days. They lived in concrete boxes. The system of teaching younger species of this race was not to stick their heads into the little black boxes so that they should learn elementary computer making and so forth, but, and this is the strange part, but to send them to enormous concrete boxes where they would sit on pieces of wood which came from *tree. . . tree* (which, I might add, has not been seen since the great disaster). And then the older species would talk to them and then the younger species would write it all down and memorise it all. They would even learn about the things a man wrote hundreds of years before that time. Funny, that . . . very funny!'

We represented the Supermarket as a salvaged piece of old film. It ran at three different speeds – and backwards as well, and we ruined a recording of *William Tell* accompanying it. The movement was deliberately formalised, rather like a dance routine, and presented, and received, as a joke in movement. In fact, we all found this idea so much fun that we dealt with the idea of commuters rather in the same way:

'And then, there was the daily migration. Commuting, this ceremonial was called. At the same time each morning, a collective urge to move seemed to overcome the males of the species, and they would gather in certain places, all dressed alike, wearing round black helmets and carrying strange weapons, one end curved, the other pointed . . .'

We showed the commuters, to some of Lumbye's 'Tivoli' music, as a dance routine, directed by Lisann Bird, who had a lot of experience with musical comedy. The steps were simple, but nevertheless the whole effect was one of a chorus routine from a musical show. This kind of work was completely different from the rest of our freely developed Dance Drama work and the children – boys as well as girls – enjoyed it tremendously as a complete change from the rest of the work they did.

At first, I had an ambivalent attitude to this work; it was obvious that the children enjoyed doing it, and when shown it was popular. But I wondered. It had, by its very nature, to be imposed work. It was, too, open to the criticism that it was frivolous. However, the more I considered it, the more I came to the conclusion that it made a useful contrast to the freer work, which it complemented; that it gave pleasure was important, too; also, it was a developing idea – the children came to use these routines in their plays – *Oh, Oh, Oh, Petruchio*, a musical version of *The Taming of the Shrew*, gained greatly from set routine dances. And by the time we came to my last production there the children were devising their own routines and thoroughly enjoying doing so.

In my early doubts there was, too, an element of puritanism. I felt instinctively that Dance Drama work should essentially be serious and my early Dance Drama work had tended to be all on the same level of intensity – a mistake, for both the players and those watching need periods of relief. It is, too, a mistake to believe that movement or dance work should only be used to convey solemn ideas solemnly: the work of Marcel

Marceau, ballets such as *Rodeo* or *La Fille Mal Gardée* are only a few instances of gaining from humour and lightness of approach. To keep only to darker tones is limiting, and often a comment can be more telling if made in a light-hearted way.

After the humour, we turned again to darker aspects of ritual: 'A strange people. I think it may have been their strangeness which led to the great disaster. You may not believe it but, in the same way that we communicate love, they actually communicated an emotion long since outlawed which was known as hatred. It was hatred which led to the great disaster. You may well wonder how it was that such a thing as hatred came to flourish. This was because men learned to control the emotions of others. It was not until people realised the dangers of this that the disaster ended and our new era began.'

The mood darkened and we showed some scenes derived from the exercises in which one person controlled another's action and those in which groups menaced or mounted attacks on one person, though without touching him. As these scenes reached a point of considerable intensity the folk songs started. Relaxation followed; the mood became gentler; then, a growing towards intensifying light – in fact, the scene which had come into being in the gym during a Club session.

I have mentioned how moving the audience found this and I feel that their response was conditioned at least in part by their reaction to the intensity of the earlier scenes. Adults sometimes find it disturbing to see children acting out scenes in which death, hatred or violence appear. We tend to be engrossed by the innocence of the world of children and do not wish our image of that world to be disturbed by darker aspects. But children, especially those approaching or passing through adolescence, are of course aware of these aspects. When one remembers the origins of Drama in the creating of a safe magic situation in which to act out dangers and release fears, and when one sees younger children spontaneously acting out scenes of great violence and carnage, it is difficult to maintain the belief that children's Drama should only be concerned with the sweet, light and innocent aspects of life. One should not draw too close a parallel between the 'Bang! You're dead! Count ten' sort of child's play and the more complex and emotionally heightened work in a Dance Drama such as *Ritual*. Of course, adolescent children vary markedly in their involvement in such a piece of work and their response to it; and the effect which they produce is often one of intensity far beyond that of their own commitment. The maturity of an audience colours its reactions, as we see in the Infant Nativity Play when the toddler with an insecure halo, propelled from the wings, rather lost but remembering just enough to run through the simple actions in which he has been drilled, can produce an overwhelming effect on those watching, without in any way attempting to do so. It is the audience, not the child, which is lapped in sentimentality. Inevitably, sensitive, perceptive adolescents will become aware of an effect or an emotion engendered, but when one sees them follow a deeply felt moment like the one which arose from the folk tunes with a riot of uninhibited activity and noise, one feels that tension has been released, it is clear, it is over. The dangers have been acted out and the catharsis has been valuable. Further observation of the children certainly confirms this initial impression. I do not believe that one must be serious or intense all the time, but equally I do not believe that serious treatment of serious themes should be avoided. On the contrary, it can be of great value.

Dance Drama *Man/Animal*

In *Space* we developed a continuous narrative from our exercises; in *Ritual*, the original ideas came in the Club sessions and then were developed in a number of other subjects, the final performance being in two portions with a fair thread of narrative, though this became tenuous at times. Because the work did not develop a story line easily or naturally, there had to be more staff selection for, and shaping of, the final work. However, it had the advantage that it saw the beginning of work interrelated with other subjects. In *Man/Animal,* we selected our general theme first, announced it to the staff as well as to the members of the Club and thereafter the work developed through reciprocal stimuli. We did not attempt any sort of continuous narrative; the theme was in itself strong enough to carry through the whole work with a feeling of homogeneity. The idea was to draw parallels between the behaviour and attitudes of man and animal. As ideas came from other lessons, we developed them, where we could, in the Club sessions; where ideas came from the Club work, we passed them on to other staff. This was done by a series of information sheets sent out to the staff. Here is the first:

'This term I would like, as on previous occasions, to use Drama work as the focus of quite a lot of related work in other subjects. The week following Open Evening will be given up to the showing of plays, films and Dance Drama, with some of the Open Evening exhibitions left up to supplement and illustrate the performances.

'*Second Year Dance Drama.* This will draw parallels between various aspects of animal and human behaviour. We have started on this in ordinary Drama Club sessions. For example: two cockerels fight to dominate the farmyard while the hens flutter round; then, in a teen-age group, two highly-coloured characters fight to be top man of the group, In each, the defeated one is spurned. Another example: poodles and their owners go for grooming; patterns of behaviour merge, and they change roles. In another scene, victims are selected by groups of predators and destroyed. We have not yet worked on a human parallel for this, but no doubt one will occur. We have also worked on improvised scenes in which the 'speech' consists entirely of animal noises. These have been very funny, but I think the idea can be sharpened and developed further. Ideas welcome. Indeed, we would very much welcome from children or from staff any other parallels which suggest themselves.

'*Wanted: Poems and dialogue on these themes.* I suggest that we do as we did before and gather blocks of children to watch the working of some of the ideas, then to discuss and to produce related writings.

'*Paintings of animals.* Collage would be particularly effective for some, perhaps. Any chance of paintings which either show animals in human conditions or vice versa? The circus work in film which Jean has been doing would also relate here.

'*Head-dresses, masks, wings for animals and birds.* Preferably in a range of media – I would particularly like wings that make use of a range of materials – cloth, plastic, foil etc.

'The Dance Drama is never "set" until the actual performance. It should grow all the time, stimulating – and being stimulated by – related work in other subjects . . .'

From this beginning, ideas began to flow back and forth. One English class developed the idea of animal speech and devised a very funny debate in the House of Commons with it, finishing with MP's being driven baa-ing into the lobbies; a History class considered early man and pointed to the idea that he was at that stage at least merely one animal among others. Their work on this and on primitive cave paintings led to a scene based on primitive man's pre-hunting rituals. Music – the opening of *La Fille Mal Gardée* – was offered to one group who used it for the cockerel scene, producing a light, neat and amusing piece of stylised movement. Other children then produced tie-and-dye wings and head-dresses for the hens, others produced paintings and screen prints on the theme. More work in the gym produced a sequence in which an inadvertent interloper into a wrestling ring is hurled about by the irate wrestlers. The interloper was very light and agile (and courageous), and the sequence, impeccably timed by the group which had devised it, scared the audiences (which pleased the group no end). One group, developing the 'parrot' idea, devised scenes in which all the dialogue was taken from television commercials. More Drama than Dance in that instance. In fact the whole approach was far more flexible now. Ideally, in a less structured situation, the children would have been able to move from one aspect of their theme to another – writing, painting, modelling, listening to music, making music. Even so, without a true inter-disciplinary situation, we nevertheless achieved a great deal of cross-fertilisation of ideas, Unfortunately, we produced no original music this time, but in the primitive man sequence we tried giving each performer a half-full match box. We first spent some time experimenting with the various sounds which could be produced from these, rattling them softly, shaking them continuously or sharply or suddenly; we even found that there was a noticeable difference in the sound produced by shaking them from side to side from that produced by shaking them from end to end, We also found that it was advisable to guard against the inside of the box flying out and dispersing its contents all over the area and its occupants. The results were interesting enough, but it would have been better if we had had more time to have explored the idea further. At a later youth drama school, I did, and was further convinced that this was something which could be most fruitfully developed, trying out all sorts of different improvised percussion instruments.

One great disappointment was that we could not include film. A group of about a dozen children had produced their own twenty-minute mock melodrama in 16-mm colour about the adventures of 'the Chameleon', a hero who could change his disguises instantaneously. They used a lot of ingenious trick photography, only some of which I saw, for the film was stolen, with the camera, when the school was broken into and we had neither the time nor the resources to remake it.

This was a long way from the early Dance Drama, in which I had been careful to ensure that the action was carried forward entirely through movement, in which it was the narrative or the sequence of ideas which governed the development of the work and predisposed its shape. Now the approach was far more flexible, taking stimulus from a range of other media and feeding stimulus into an increasing range of subjects as well as stating a point of view. Certainly no longer 'pure' Dance Drama. But it was accepted quite naturally as another medium in which to present ideas, not only by those who took part in the Drama Club or productions but by all the children. It was not thought

of as precious or esoteric – certainly not when most of the
Rugby First XV took part with obvious enjoyment and lack
of self-consciousness. It had become a central part of school
life.

Chapter 7

Impetus

My general aim had been to give the children as wide an experience as possible over as wide a range as possible, with the implied assumption that they would be given, and be capable of taking, the chance of using this experience to develop work and ideas of their own. However, faced with this first 'sixth form', I realised that my thinking had not been sufficiently detailed. I suppose this was inevitable, because it is difficult to project one's thinking into a future situation, as yet ill-defined. I had not, for instance, taken into account the extra facilities offered by the growth of Youth Wing activities. Now, we had a newly appointed Youth Tutor, establishing his Youth Wing to make a bridge between school life and work and those of the community at large. For the first time it was possible to organise official, subsidised classes or activities – in Drama, among other things.

Because I was enthusiastically committed to work in Drama, I tended to overlook the fact that it took a great deal of time, especially with the intensive approach to the production of plays. Generally, half-term weeks were completely taken up with the demands of an impending production; often, many evenings of the week would be filled with work on other aspects. And those adults who were willing to tackle drama work in the way to which I was committed, whether working on a Dance Drama or a movement sequence for a production or a relatively conventional production, inevitably found that this made considerable demands on their time and energy. So I felt it only fair, once it became possible for them to be paid as Youth Wing instructors, that they should be. It is easy enough in education to exploit

134

people because of their dedication, expecting them to put on plays, run teams, organise activities. I am not against dedication; quite the contrary. But, although I personally prefer not to undertake official courses because I don't like being committed in that particular way, I hold that it is not reasonable to assume that the only possible reward for someone who gives up much spare time, expends much energy and undergoes considerable nervous strain, is the satisfaction of knowing that he has done his bit. Obviously, that is a great part of the reward, but it will not be devalued by some additional incentive (which is often rather meagre, anyway).

I had vaguely assumed that our new senior pupils, when they came of age, would create their own structure within which all sorts of exciting dramatic activities would flourish. I had not even been very clear about this: all I had assumed was that, having cleared 'O' levels and being therefore in some way translated, they would now all automatically start to put forth dramatic blossoms without further prompting from me. Although not completely unjustified, this was nevertheless an over-optimistic view. I had given them the equipment, the incentive, but not the organisation.

This was partly a reflection of my own temperament and approach. Tackling productions as I did, I had not the time for lengthy planning or publicity. Any advance information tended to be very vague, and on calendars of coming events which we sent out to parents and other interested people the only information about Drama was in vague terms such as 'projected Main Production' or 'on one of the evenings of Open Week we shall be showing what Drama and allied work we have to hand by then'. I found it hard to be tied firmly to one week, decided well in advance, for our double Shakespeare productions. Up till this time, all the threads had been more or less held in my own hands, but from this time on all sorts of different people – Youth Wing groups, sixth formers, specialist groups, *ad hoc* collections of people who wished to put on a particular play – would be initiating projects and someone, or some central body, would have to co-ordinate these. So I launched 'Impetus' and signalled the occasion by issuing an explanatory 'hand-out', although normally in a large school where communication could become deadly synonymous with bits of paper this was something I preferred not to do.

What is IMPETUS?

We have a number of Senior Drama activities in progress at school at the moment: two Youth Drama Groups (with a third projected); various Main Productions, especially those involving the fifth and sixth forms; groups working on poetry readings, setting music to words and words to music, designing settings for production, working on experiments in movement and lighting; working on other technical aspects of stagecraft. We have gathered all these activities together, under the name of IMPETUS and organised by a group of senior pupils. A number of members of staff are also involved in the work, producing, advising, taking part. From time to time, IMPETUS will stage major productions, and sometimes there will be informal evenings when work in progress will be shown to invited audiences.

On December 3rd we are holding the first of our informal IMPETUS evenings, in which we will show some of the work that is in progress at the moment, including an experiment in movement, devised by some sixth formers; another experiment involving lighting and music, devised by some other sixth formers; improvisation by members of the Youth Drama; poetry reading – and anything else which has happened by that time.

IMPETUS ACTIVITIES NEXT TERM

January 17th	Poetry recital
January 24th	Programme of One Act Plays
January 31st	*The Italian Straw Hat* (First Youth Drama Group)

February 14th-21st	Third and Fourth Year Main Productions (Two productions, on alternate nights, of *A Midsummer Night's Dream* – not IMPETUS activities)
February 28th	Strindberg's *Miss Julie* (Workshop production)
March 6th	Pinter's *The Dumb Waiter*
March 7th	IMPETUS evening
March 13th	Youth Drama Festival
March 20th	*Reluctant Heroes*

Although circumstances required that the ultimate clearing of bookings and dates had to be done through me, I did, as the hand-out indicates, set up a committee which did a lot of the rest of the work. This was very much an *ad hoc* affair as there was at that time no larger official body which could nominate or elect such a committee. Later, there was a School Council which might perhaps have done this. As it was, I gathered together an initial group which represented a wide range of interests, making sure that particular areas, especially particular academic areas, were not over heavily represented. This committee, like all things organic, immediately began to change and develop as some people became less interested and others took their place. I had a somewhat unformulated idea that ultimately this committee should become entirely responsible for the organisation and co-ordination of all Impetus activities, but I knew they would first need experience of the problems. Gradually, areas evolved where the responsibility was taken over by the committee or some members of it.

The school system for the co-ordination of dates precluded them from dealing with this particular aspect. Main production dates, especially for the third and fourth year children, were governed by external factors: dates of exams, Sports Days and other school events, They were, therefore, generally the first to be fixed. Then the official youth groups preferred to have fixed dates to work towards; on the example list, their productions were *The Italian Straw Hat* and *Reluctant Heroes* (they

K

were not always light-hearted, but tackled a good range of plays). Individuals and small groups, such as the one producing *The Dumb Waiter*, then asked for the dates and made their selection from what was available. On other 'blanket' dates such as 'Impetus evenings', anyone who happened to have anything of interest ready could contribute. Before long, it became regular practice for any groups of senior pupils who so wished to initiate their own productions, from *The Caretaker* to *Coriolanus*. My own function was to indicate limitations on rehearsal facilities and to arrange a date for production. Inevitably, this was done, indeed had to be done, as a straightforward administrative matter based on cold practical considerations; it was not possible to plan an aesthetically balanced 'season'.

Some of the projects did not succeed. The poetry recital mentioned on the list came to nothing, despite the fact that the selection of readings was careful and interesting, because the initiators of the idea relied too much on me for arranging practical matters such as typing and duplicating the poems, arranging publicity and so on. I was short of time, and the jobs were not done efficiently, or not done at all. A more ambitious undertaking, a production of *Coriolanus*, also failed to materialise, but those responsible for initiating that project learned a great deal about organising rehearsal schedules and ensuring that their cast observed them. They, also learned something about their own limitations; and having learned, moved on successfully to tackle other exciting undertakings.

The frequency of performances inevitably meant an overall diminution in the size of audiences. I felt that this was of little importance, generally. A number of workshop performances were given quite informally to small, invited audiences. Those taking part had the pleasure of bringing their work to the stage where it could be performed, shared with interested people, and often discussed with them afterwards. There was an implicit understanding on the scale of each undertaking; in the given list, for instance, the main productions and youth group productions played to large audiences and made satisfying profits. The others played to far smaller audiences – in one instance, less than two dozen – but these were enthusiastic and constructively critical. We had an understanding that, whereas individual productions could be subsidised from school funds, Drama as a whole was expected to pay in more than it took out. This was not difficult, for main productions, particularly those with very large casts of young children, whose relations packed the halls, generally made an excellent profit. They could therefore subsidise the less profitable ventures. Anyway, the profit motive is not invariably the best one for putting on a production: with amateur groups, I generally found that it was far easier to make money by putting on a Jumble Sale. The profits from this enabled one to tackle a play one wanted to do, without having to worry about whether it would make money or not.

The committee dealt manfully with increasing areas of organisation, but it would have been far better had I possessed the facility to develop a really efficient central organisation. As this was not one of my strengths, we tended to manage, rather than to deal very efficiently with problems. We also suffered from the lack of a central organisation for properties, sets and costumes; indeed, we suffered very much from the lack of any sort of proper storage facilities for costumes or scenery. In effect, our only real storage space was the stage itself, unusable for this purpose while productions were in preparation or being presented. Ideally what we needed, and what I would have had to persuade myself to organise had I stayed in that particular post, would have been a separate, central system for dealing with the practicalities of mounting a large number of plays, under a permanent Productions Manager, who was not personally involved in any of the groups or productions.

A permanent Productions Manager, or preferably, Production Managing team, could have taken over the responsibility for the care, storage and maintenance of scenery, properties and costumes. He – or they – would have then been able to draw up realistic schedules for setting the productions and, what is perhaps more important to general ease of running, for striking the sets. As it was, the tight schedule we worked to did in itself impose certain rather tight limitations. It was never possible,

except with the first production in any term, to start putting
up a set until a date fairly close to the date of production. I had
to take care to leave reasonable time before any production
(such as *A Midsummer Night's Dream* on the hand-out list)
which required a rather more elaborate setting, or one which
took longer to put up, or one (a multi-purpose set for *View
From the Bridge*, for instance) which required that rehearsals
should take place on the actual setting. However, one couldn't
always start work on the date one expected to if, for instance,
the team responsible for the previous production had heartily
celebrated their success and retired leaving the acting area a
shambles. On such occasions, I tried to persuade myself to
balance the value of giving actors experience in all the practical
work so that, at least in part, they lost the impression that they
were rather beautiful and special people, with the annoyance,
frustration and sheer temper aroused when a group in fact
acted according to that impression. Then, I felt strongly that
it would have been far better to have had the area neatly
cleared, swept and made ready by a team which might not
necessarily have had any personal interest in the production.
As it was, the striking of settings was sometimes performed
meticulously; sometimes rather scantily or not at all. Sometimes, with apparent efficiency, the area would be left clear,
beautifully swept, neat and tidy, and only gradually would one
realise that though the clearing had indeed been efficiently
done, replacing had not. Curtains had been removed and mis-
laid, all sorts of modifications had been made to the runners
and tracks, all the overhead lighting had been transferred to
ground level and remained there, and so on. After one Shakespeare production, in which banners swung superbly into place,
we were never again able to use the standard curtain setting
supplied with the stage because of irreversible modifications to
curtains and tracks.

Another thing a Production Manager might have been more
successful at was in preventing modifications to standard pieces
of setting. One production had planned to make use of white
screens for its setting and was placed in great difficulty by

140

another group who borrowed the screens for a production of *Stop it, Whoever You Are* and transformed them, with the use of creosote, it seemed, to lavatory doors. Much later, when the screens were painted over for other settings, forest glades or eastern temples, the stark words 'GENTS, NUMBER ONE', would somehow make their way to the surface. This sort of thing, I should emphasise, was by no means common practice, but when it did happen it led to great irritation and took me from the business of Drama, in which I was interested, into the sphere of administration and planning, in which I was nothing like so interested.

Most productions had efficient business management, though publicity was variable; and in any case, audiences tended, as I have said, to be small except for major performances. It was always impressive to see a Youth Wing production wholly managed by fifth or sixth formers with both efficiency and profitability. All productions employed the same general procedure for booking and seat reservations, which was useful. Though it was sometimes not followed, a clear system for liaison between consecutive productions soon evolved, as did a system for notifying our regular followers, who received, generally termly, hand-outs like the one I have included, on forthcoming Drama work. (At the time that particular notice was issued, the normally flourishing PTA Drama Group was going through a period of debility, otherwise information about its productions was normally included: generally one major production and one workshop piece or less ambitious production each term.) We evolved a somewhat *ad hoc* method for paying for commonly-used stock – bulbs for the stage lighting, for instance, were not only expensive, but always seemed to give up immediately before one of my own productions. People were very good about keeping to their dates, as indeed they had to be; only once did a production turn rogue and lurch erratically through a range of dates, cutting across other projects and indeed obliterating one of my own productions completely. It was not one of my favourite Shakespeare plays, either: *A Winter's Tale*, which blighted three other seasons.

I wanted to signal the start of 'Impetus' with something a bit special. Some of the pupils – and staff – particularly interested in Drama had begun to talk about the possibility of making our own full-length group play. One colleague, Enid Parker, who was a prime mover in this project, generously offered a strong and interesting theme *The Sword* on which she had been working, on and off, for a number of years. It seemed to me to be not only challenging but also sufficiently flexible to allow for considerable development and change, if the occasion arose. It was also immediately obvious that the idea strongly engaged the interest and enthusiasm of the sixth formers with whom I started work on the play.

At that time, I was of the opinion that efficiency and democracy were both best served by setting up a committee (or more than one, if possible). I therefore asked a collection of pupils to form a 'Sword' Committee. I tried to represent various facets, the costume designers, musicians, writers, scenery designers and builders as well as the performers. A few lost their enthusiasm and drifted off the committee, but others drifted on to take their places. In any case, once the project was under way, the individual members of the committee carried on dealing with their particular areas of responsibility on their own, calling on me for help only on the odd occasions when they could not resolve a difficulty.

The important ingredient for the success of the idea was the enthusiasm of those involved in the project. It could well have been that, though the project enthused me, it produced little or no response from the pupils with whom I hoped to develop it. It is certainly possible to push through a Drama project without the deep commitment of all those involved in it; even, to produce a technically expert result, well-liked and acclaimed. But I knew that this might well mean working without enthusiasm and pleasure. I knew, too, that it would be very hard work, unfamiliar and therefore worrying to me, and quite possibly a failure in performance. I determined, therefore, that the project should at least be pleasurable.

What we had to begin with was an idea, supplemented by

some fragments of dialogue, and some suggestions as to how the idea might be established and developed. We spent a lot of the earlier sessions improvising episodes in the first half, which established the dilemma and the response of the characters to that dilemma. The dramatic scenes were far easier to improvise and gave more satisfaction, to those watching as well as to those taking part, than lyrical, sentimental or expository episodes.

When a scene went well and we were all satisfied with its content and style we then had to decide how to preserve it. Sometimes we decided not to record it in any way, but to leave it to the players to reproduce when necessary. This was generally easier in long speeches, in duologues, and especially in situations where forcefulness would more than compensate for any roughness. Poetic utterances needed more polishing or preparation.

One of my tasks was to keep an eye on the overall shape of each sequence. We had decided on a general pattern: a Prelude – a blood sacrifice – followed by the First Movement, which would establish the conflict between the advocates of peace and those of the Sword. In the Second Movement, this conflict would grow into crisis, followed by confrontation, then resolution.

I must not, however, give the impression that the work developed in an orderly fashion with one scene growing naturally as soon as the preceding one was moulded to everyone's satisfaction. Indeed, it is impossible to remember clearly exactly how things did develop. People kept coming up with ideas; some scenes whose outline had been agreed simply did not work out in practice; other scenes were quietly developing on their own, without a great deal of communication with the rest of the project.

It was interesting to see how an excellently strong and dramatic idea, suggested by the original author at a time when she was not directly concerned with the performers, simply did not satisfy those who had now identified themselves with the characters. I was frequently reminded of Pirandello's *Six Char-*

acters in Search of an Author. The priest of an idolatrous sect could not reconcile himself to a cold-blooded killing; to him, it seemed too melodramatically villainous. But, as a believer in the divinity of his golden idol, he felt that the profanation of that idol would provide the strongest possible motivation. The dominant wife of the king, required to engineer a plot, found that her function lacked subtlety. She needed a chance fusion of motive and opportunity which readily suggested itself and made a previously thin part of the play not only more dramatic but far more credible. A blind beggar became fascinated by the involvement of his character in events in which he could not actively participate. Until that time, he had tended to be a vague, peripheral character, adding a little colour to the scene. But he now became aware of the danger for him in the fact that events could be discussed or enacted in his presence, disregarded at the time, but, when reflected on, placing him at great risk, particularly considering his vulnerability.

It would have been relatively quick and simple to have arranged for a small committee to sort out the plot of the Second Movement and draw up an outline on which we could all have worked. As it happened, we took a far more exhausting and potentially irritating approach. We tried to settle it in open session, starting the Second Movement with the characters involved trying to work their way through, and a rather large group of other characters, friends, interested parties, bystanders, technicians, staff and so on contributing their ideas. The session lasted hours. A number of people nearly came to blows. Some of the cast almost reached a state of schizophrenia, arguing sometimes as themselves, sometimes as the characters they were playing. Other people contributed a mixture of comment and performance. Sometimes, the large group broke up into a lot of smaller ones, arguing, discussing, improvising, jotting down ideas. Inevitably, the dual tension led to bathetic moments. The groping beggar had his hand trodden on and produced a strong and fluent improvisation which reflected more of his Rugby background than his ancient civilisation doppelganger.

Eventually, quite a measure of agreement was reached. It is impossible to remember how, but somehow it came about. Perhaps it was exhaustion. At the time, all I felt was utter tiredness and some irritation at the time it had all taken. On reflection, I am fascinated by the complexity of the process by which all those involved reached a resolution of their problems which satisfied them both as individuals and as performers.

At the next working session, because of all the work we had put into the resolution of the ideas, we were able to establish without much difficulty the whole of the Second Movement. There was remarkable unanimity, almost telepathy, at times. Sometimes, the idea would spark out from a number of different places at the same time; sometimes, people would find themselves accepting a point and taking it one stage further without actually hearing it put into words.

At that session, we settled almost all our problems, except how to end the play. We were now very close indeed to the performance dates, and we felt we needed at least one full run through before sharing the work with an audience, so it was necessary to reach a decision at one final working session.

By now, real life and involvement in the drama were becoming intermingled. The principals were much exhausted by the extent of their participation, but a new group was becoming involved – people playing the Citizens, who had begun to take more and more part in the work sessions, and to alter the intensity or even the character of the scene by their participation. I don't quite know how it came about, but we found that numbers of those involved, sometimes people who had not previously shown a great deal of interest in Drama, began to dominate the discussions and markedly to affect the development of the final resolution. In the performance, the major characters took no further part in the action after the final crisis. Only Heth, the leader and major character, added his final comment, left alone in the acting area, irresolute, unable to decide whether to follow his people or remain in his deserted city, inhabited only by memories and the body of his son.

This solution came after another intensive work session. It was not reached easily, or without living through a number of simulated situations which could have followed the final crisis. The reaction of each major character was discussed and resolved. Many possibilities were tested and rejected. The Citizens dominated the end of the play in reality and in the action. Derek/Heth could not alter their decision; could not bring himself to go with them; could not longer dictate the course of events.

We just had time before the performances to work out the Prologue, the ritual killing, which, paradoxically, lightened the prevailing intensity in that all those concerned gained great pleasure from Movement work, and some of those who had been talked down in discussions were, in this different context, able to reassert themselves.

There are so many different ways of going about the making of a group play. One could start with the actual 'performance' itself, involving the audience in the discussion and the making of the scenes and incidents. This requires a special type of audience, though. It could be dispiriting, to say the least, to launch that sort of enterprise with an audience which settled into rigid embarrassment and fixed grins. (And, anyway, I have a perhaps old-fashioned belief that it is discourteous to embarrass one's audience.) There could, certainly, be far less structuring of scenes. This would undoubtedly give greater spontaneity, but it also involves greater risk. It is quite possible for a player to be carried away, to speak and act inconsistently, to produce moments of high drama which, although perhaps highly effective, were false within the situation. It would also be possible for the whole thing to degenerate into giggles, tedium and disappointment. I have seen that happen, too.

I suppose one's approach must be governed largely by the extent of the risk that one is willing (or able) to undertake and, most important of all, by the inclinations of the group who are going to work on the project. It is perfectly possible to produce an 'improvisation' in the creating of which the players have had almost no say; the producer can dictate it, scene by scene. This often produces quick and effective results, immediate euphoria, but ultimate disillusion.

If a group has worked together a great deal, and particularly if it has done a lot of improvised drama, the members can often achieve a remarkable empathy and produce results which are very smooth and attractive. Sometimes, this is a good thing; sometimes it means that they are no longer much involved, but are working to a pattern, very much, I suppose, as the original Commedia dell'Arte players did. Certainly, anyone who is undertaking this kind of work can gain from a study of Commedia dell'Arte, which can enrich one's approach to a wide variety of plays.

One of the drawbacks, for an author, of using his idea as the basis for a group play-making project is that, once the idea is committed to the group, it belongs to them and not to the originator (or the director of the project, for that matter). Fortunately, the provider of the idea readily accepted that it was likely to be knocked around and radically changed; that pieces of dialogue presented with the original idea were likely to be rewritten or amended beyond recognition. However, although she attended almost all of *The Sword* working sessions and participated actively, she did so simply as one of the group, claiming no special consideration.

Later, she wrote: 'What fascinates is the richness of the children's characterisation within the suggested framework, which they enlarged by new characters and new situations which in turn enriched and improved the original plot. The experience of sitting-in on rehearsals and watching the cast bring a real play to life, to hear them improvising, cutting, firing, moulding the play until the end that had seemed hopeless burst out in the last couple of days – it was all a remarkable, indeed unique, experience, for me, at least. . . .'

The Sword was a success at all levels, probably fortuitously. But it took me some time to recover from the sheer exhaustion brought about by the way we tackled it. I have done quite a lot of similar work since, though. It has been much less exhausting, but has somehow left me less exhilarated. One develops short cuts, formulae, to avoid the exhaustion. Inevitably, I fear, they eliminate some of the exhilaration, too.

Conclusion

It was interesting – and rather gratifying – to see how the staff gradually began to accept and make use of the fact that the children had facility in Drama and enjoyed using it. For them, it had become a fully acceptable way of presenting information, ideas, interpretation. In the general life of the school we became so used to the confidence and articulateness of the children that we tended to take it for granted until visitors commented on it: some even suspected that, in some way, this impression was produced by sleight of hand. We had a great many groups of visitors, and when one of these arrived I would catch hold of the nearest children who were available, perhaps those unable to do Games on that day, for instance, and simply ask them to take the visitors around wherever they wanted to go (and, if they hadn't any particular preferences, to suggest an itinerary), explaining the school to them and answering their questions. One such group of visitors found it difficult to accept that the children had not been specially selected – not exactly injected with cold virus, or having had their kit incinerated, but nevertheless told to stand by to receive visitors. Others accepted the accidental nature of the selection, but took it for granted that this was a random selection from the academically more able, believing, as do a number of people, that the child who for some reason cannot read or write fluently necessarily cannot express himself with oral fluency. These children believed, as I do, that children should not only be heard but listened to. And, just as I believe that children should not be talked down to, so I do not believe they should be listened down to; it worries me to see the child who is encouraged by grown-up company to be pert, precious or precocious. I find it difficult to approve of adults who expect, or worse, encourage,

children to act and talk like the synthetic juveniles in television commercials; nor do I find commendable a school
situation which may be thought to be relaxed and informal, but
where a fundamental unease over relationships results in a lot
of brash banter or a lot of good-natured sound but precious
little communication.

A number of subjects made much use of Drama, not as a
relaxation only marginally more justifiable than letting the
children play noughts and crosses, but as an integral part of the
course. The teaching of foreign languages was based on an oral
approach – we had been a centre for a Nuffield pilot scheme and
were equipped with language laboratories. Very soon, the children acquired not only their basic vocabulary but also the
conversation necessary to build up short scenes. For example,
in one situation, the family assembled for breakfast and the
postman arrived with a parcel. What it contained was not
specified. All the children acted out their scenes with vitality –
if the girl playing the mother was required to chide her tardy
son, or her children were to express approval or disapproval of
the food, it would not occur to them to use intonations less
true to life than they would in any of their other Drama work.
This gave vitality and naturalness to their speaking of the
language. The open-ended nature of the scene gave the children
plenty of opportunity for development: they could, if they
wished, simply mime the contents of the parcel for the rest to
name (in the appropriate language, of course) or they could
name it and talk about it, using language they had already
acquired: 'It is beautiful!', 'Give it to me', and so on.

Later, some of the children became adept at melding two
or three different dialogues together to make one long and quite
complex scene, often adding phrases which they got from their
teacher. Other classes worked as a group, putting together
whole scenes, taking an everyday situation as the basis of their
work. I remember one in particular, spoken with life, fluency
and accuracy by the 'least able' linguists. It was set in a
grocery and finished with a spectacular collapse of tins (brought
from home) as the fussy old lady selected the one she wanted

from the bottom of an elaborate display. This upset her so much that she left without buying anything after all. I laughed at all the funny bits. The children were a bit surprised and somewhat suspicious as I was not a French teacher, and therefore was presumably ignorant of the language. I think they thought that I had been specially primed, and probably nudged at the appropriate moments. This was, of course, a group taken by a teacher who believed in this approach; any teacher who felt uneasy about the use of acting would almost inevitably transmit that unease to the children and produce dull work which could be instanced to support the unease which had led to it, thus producing more unease, duller work, and so on. If a teacher is not committed to this approach, it is probably better for him not to use it at all.

On Open Evenings, the language rooms were fully occupied for the entire time with shadow plays, puppet plays and live performances. The interesting part of all this was the audience, who reacted with understanding and appreciation to scenes performed in languages which many of them could understand only a little, or not at all – French, Spanish, Russian. But the words were delivered so meaningfully that the audience could understand what was happening.

Even with a committed teacher, the use of Drama had its dangers. Dramatic effect and sober truth are not always reconcilable, and this was sometimes apparent in History work. I remember seeing a small group presenting a simple and historically accurate little scene, which they had researched themselves, about seventeenth century parents instructing their children in their duties and obligations. The rest of the children watched it respectfully, but without enthusiasm. It was informative, accurate, worthy, but not really interesting. Another group, though, rocked with delight at a ribald sketch about Henry VIII and an indeterminate number of wives. It was no more true to life (or less funny, it is fair to say) than the average television sketch. The children enjoyed it whole-heartedly, but it can have done nothing but damage to their sense of historical perspective.

151

Certainly, the first was more true to its material; the second was better entertainment. What both lacked was the teacher's part in putting the work into perspective, and probably in helping to prepare the work itself, for this was, after all, Drama used for a special purpose. Many teachers still feel that, even if the material is being drawn from their subject and the result presented in their lesson, because it is Drama, they are not qualified (or allowed) to tamper with it. The Drama mystique remains strong, and sometimes militates against the wider use of Drama in education. In the first play, extensive source material was available – in itself most valuable – but the teacher had left the children to work completely on their own and had not encouraged them to use their dialogue as meaningfully as with the essentially simpler dialogues of a French lesson, for instance. In the second play, a lively group had been given its head because the teacher did not feel that he could interfere with the creative process and so had not liked to remind them that they should retain respect for both medium and message.

In Science, short plays were introduced into the work schedules, illustrating some events in the lives of great scientists, dramatising great discoveries and so on. As this happened just before I left, I did not have time to gain any real impression of their effectiveness. I have always tended to mistrust encapsulated 'Great moments from . . .', for I have not come across many which convey a sense of reality, perhaps because they do not usually have sufficient time to establish characters and situations before jerking rapidly into the 'Pierre, a wonderful thing has happened – I have discovered Radium!' situation. Even so, I was glad to find that Drama had infiltrated the teaching of a subject not traditionally associated with it. One Geographer tentatively used the same sort of approach to illustrate Life in Other Lands, but without a great deal of success. Again, shorter scenes gave the children little sense of reality, and a worthy desire to impart a lot of information, and not to waste too much time on the dramatic trimmings tended to lead to a wooden dialogue which, delivered in a rather uninvolved way by the children who had had their requests to be allowed to 'liven it up a bit' turned down, tended to produce giggles rather than absorbed interest. This confirmed the teacher's view that Drama was essentially a flippant enterprise, inappropriate to a serious learning situation.

This view was countered in Religious Education. Again, it would have been possible to have prepared dull little playlets on Abraham and Isaac, or Victorian parables about the inevitable rewards of virtue. Fortunately, that did not happen. If one is not too restricted by the syllabus, there is much excellent material available, for instance in the Miracle and Mystery plays. The Cain and Abel sequence in the Wakefield Mystery Cycle proved a wonderful stimulus for children in groups I have worked with; they readily found modern parallels, producing dramatic confrontations between the aggressive, less privileged youngster and the more conventional brother, more secure in his place in society. Then they played the two episodes, the original and the modern version, one after the other, finding each one thoroughly absorbing, though for different reasons. Modern parallels readily caught the interest of the children. The modern versions of the parables which we used in *Pilgrim* were mainly produced as part of the Religious Education work, and were only a small selection of those written. This type of work was developed most successfully by one teacher, who frequently used *Pilgrim* as her starting point. One of her groups re-worked the Good Samaritan parable from the play, bringing in a Pakistani, and presented it as part of a school assembly, working carefully on preparation and presentation. Other, more impromptu offerings were fairly often worked out by children without staff assistance. These tended to carry their point home more firmly and memorably than any homily I might deliver.

Not always, though. In our dramatic assemblies, we came up against the problem which has been with us since the times of Miracles and Moralities (and earlier than that) that the villains and devils so often seem to have far more fun than the virtuous characters. One assembly scene, designed to point the moral that it is unkind to mock your fellow pupils, succeeded, unfortunately, in making the point that it can be tremendous fun

153

to tease them, and that unkind comments can be far more amusing and enjoyable than a virtuous summing-up. Nevertheless, as a general rule, we found that the sincerity and directness of most of the assembly plays proved valuable, partly because they were plays, and the children enjoyed Drama; partly, too, because the children, brought up in an increasingly materialistic society where traditional religious ties were weakening, responded more readily to a morality expressed in everyday terms and related to a social rather than a spiritual condition.

I had become so used to Dance Dramas being developed as inter-disciplinary projects that the introduction in the curriculum of various inter-disciplinary areas seemed to me likely to prove no more than an extension of that work. But I was wrong. The thing about Dance Drama was that any department could contribute if it wished. If it did not, or was not able to, the structure was not impaired. Children would automatically use PE time, facilities, staff expertise, to work on particular sections which particularly needed those things; others would be keen to carry on developing an idea in Music, or in Art and Craft in which, often, it was possible to provide equipment or facilities over and above the usual ones available to the children. For example, quite a few of them had their first experience of batik work, tie-dye, making a large-scale or more ambitious models, because Drama work could use these and so would pay for the materials used. But, then, involvement was optional and the development organic, not closely structured. Creating a structure should not necessarily have destroyed the informal, organic quality, but in fact it did. In only one project, on Space, did the work flow easily across Drama, Music and Physical Education, the three subjects involved in this integrated situation. The children started their treatment of the theme in a Drama session, developed the movement in the gym with ingenious use of the apparatus, made or composed their own music, or listened to Richard Strauss, Morton Subotnik, Stravinsky and a number of other composers to choose their music to move to. After a while, some of them forgot which 'subject' they were involved in at any one time; for them, the boundaries had gone.

That was exceptional, though. In other instances, the structure seemed to inhibit the development of the ideas and the very stimulation of ideas which it was intended to encourage. Perhaps it would have been better simply to have planned to make it physically possible to work across the boundaries of any of the subjects, to have offered opportunities which did not have to be taken up, and waited to see what would grow from that. At any rate, it became apparent that putting three departmental cockerels into an inter-disciplinary sack and tying it up with a neat loop of time-tabling was more likely to produce disintegration than the opposite.

Fashions change in education as elsewhere. Subject boundaries change, so do approaches, techniques, content of the curriculum. So, too, do examination requirements. When I started teaching, it was rare for any school to have a Drama specialist; now, many have one, or more than one. What they do varies considerably, but it does seem that we are in a stage where the importance of Drama in schools is growing, and the subject is less often regarded as peripheral. I think it is inevitable that its function must still remain without full definition, must vary from one situation to another. This is one of the reasons why it is almost impossible to write a book about Drama.

One of my pleasures was to wander round the school at lunchtime. Often, one would come upon small groups making plays for their own pleasure, or for the enjoyment of a small collection of friends or onlookers. Sometimes, I would watch a group spending the whole of a break or their spare lunchtime in summer, out of doors, creating Drama, with others strolling by, sometimes becoming involved, sometimes watching for a while, then moving on. Much of what I have written about in this book has changed. What remains unchangeable is the love the children have for their Drama, their wholehearted commitment. While so many things change, children, thank goodness, remain essentially much the same.

155

Appendix: Useful Music

If people make suggestions about the kind of music which they think I might find useful for Drama work, I tend to be offended and to stick somewhat perversely to my own ideas. If you feel the same, I suggest that you ignore this section. I started it reluctantly, but was moved to do so by the argument that some people might find specific suggestions of value. I did not feel that a simple list without any sort of commentary would be valuable, yet I am very conscious that a list with comments may simply amount to a statement of personal preferences. But certainly it is better to follow personal preferences.

My list contains no vocal music and little chamber music. This does not mean that I believe that they should not be used, but simply that they do not usually feel right for me. I do not generally use works which have a special personal significance for me (which eliminates most of Mozart, for instance). I do not often chop bits out of symphonies, except those which are essentially programmatic, though I often break my rules by using Vaughan Williams' Sixth Symphony with its desolate last movement, and Carl Nielsen's Fifth Symphony, in the first movement of which the composer instructs the tympanist to devise a cadenza as if trying to stop the progress of the orchestra at all costs. There are no absolute criteria. With music, as with clothes, I would rather feel comfortable than correct.

I have found some pieces of music regularly useful because of the wide range of moods each contains – lyrical, dramatic, atmospheric, and so on. These I look upon as 'general purpose' records and, if I were buying just a few records to use with Drama, I would include some of these:

Drama casebook

(1) *General Purpose*

Bartok	Concerto for Orchestra
Holst	The Planets
Mussorgsky	Pictures from an Exhibition
Prokofiev	Lieutenant Kije
Rimsky Korsakov	Scheherezade
Richard Strauss	Also Sprach Zarathustra

Music which tells a tale can be very useful; it is obviously not necessary to keep to the original story, though in the following examples some may feel that the story is too strongly imprinted in the music for it to be used in any other way:

(2) *Programme Music*

Arnold	Tam O'Shanter
Bartok	Suite: The Miraculous Mandarin
Eric Coates	Cinderella
	The Three Bears
Dukas	The Sorceror's Apprentice
Saint Saens	Le Rouet D'Omphale
	Danse Macabre
Richard Strauss	Till Eulenspiegel

To someone who did not know the stories of those pieces of music they could perhaps be just as valuable for general use as the following which do not conjure up a particular story for me, but offer plenty of changes of mood, rhythm and tempo and so lend themselves to a freer interpretation:

(3) *Evocative Music*

Bax	The Garden of Fand
	Tintagel
	November Woods
Berlioz	Symphonie Fantastique
	(Especially the last two movements)
Butterworth	The Shropshire Lad

158

Debussy	La Mer
	Nocturnes
	Images
Delius	Brigg Fair
Dvořák	The Noonday Witch
	The Golden Spinning Wheel
	The Watersprite

(These charming pieces seem much at odds with the gruesome stories which they purport to tell)

Janáček	Sinfonietta
Kodály	Suite: Hary Janos
Liszt	Les Preludes
	Mazeppa

(And other symphonic poems; most symphonic poems, incidentally, prove useful)

Mussorgsky	Night on a Bare Mountain
Rachmaninov	The Isle of the Dead
Raff	Lenora Symphony
	(especially the last two movements)
Respighi	Brazilian Impressions
	Fountains of Rome
	Pines of Rome
Sibelius	Four Legends
	Finlandia
	En Saga
Tchaikovsky	Overture: Romeo and Juliet
	Overture: Hamlet
	Francesca Da Rimini
Vaughan Williams	The Lark Ascending

Ballet music was, after all, written for dancing to and, although it would be foolish to try to reproduce the originals, such music can be most valuable in Drama.

Drama casebook

(4) *Ballet Music*

Bliss	Miracle in the Gorbals
Copland	Billy the Kid
	Appalachian Spring
Prokofiev	Romeo and Juliet
	Cinderella
Stravinsky	Petrushka
	The Rite of Spring
	The Firebird
Vaughan Williams	Job, A Masque for Dancing

For many children, all music is new; they are generally un-inhibited by preconceived ideas and music which might prove daunting for some adults can be readily accepted by children, and be of great value in establishing an atmosphere.

(5) *Atmospheric Music*

Bartok	Music for Strings, Percussion and Celesta
Ives	Three Places in New England
	Thanksgiving Day
Lidholm	Rites
Messiaen	Oiseaux Exotiques
Norgaard	Constellations
Schoenberg	Serenade Opus 24
	Five Pieces for Orchestra
Varese	Ionisation
	Intégrales

There is also a great deal of electronic music now available on record. Almost any extended piece is likely to include a range of atmospheric music. I have found Morton Subotnik's 'Silver Apples of the Moon' particularly useful.

Much music of National character is dance-like. For this section, I think it would generally be more useful to indicate the type of music rather than one or two specific instances, though with one or two composers that is more appropriate.

160

(6) *Music with National Characteristics*

Arnold	especially the English and Scottish Dances
Dvořák	Slavonic Dances and other Czech music
de Falla	Spanish music
Gershwin	American in Paris, etc.
Morton Gould	another American composer
Grainger	light, attractive, evoking pastoral England
Grieg	Norwegian, making much use of folk music
Janáček	The Lachian Dances
Khatchaturian	who wrote other music as well as the Sabre Dance
Rimsky Korsakov	not only Russian music but Capriccio Espagnol, too
Virgil Thompson	who evokes pastoral USA, especially in the Louisiana Story music and The Plow that Broke the Plains
Villa Lobos	Brazilian composer

And then there are the Viennese dances of Schubert, Lanner and Mozart, the music of the Strauss family, of Offenbach and other great operetta composers.

It would be a shame, too, to ignore simply funny or light-hearted music such as:

(7) Chabrier	Marche Joyeuse
Milhaud	Le Bœuf Sur le Toit
Lumbye	Copenhagen Tivoli Music
Ibert	Divertissement
Satie	Parade
Walton	Façade

(though sense of humour varies so from one person to another)

For *Musical Portraits*, I have used Elgar's 'Enigma' Variations and invariably found that the children liked, and were intrigued by, them. Other portraits they enjoyed were: Billy Buck and Jody from Copland's *The Red Pony* music, the 'Comforters' from Vaughan Williams' *Job*, and the easy-going man from Nielsen's 'Four Temperaments' Symphony (Symphony No. 2, second movement). They also liked the brashly confident man portrayed in the fourth movement. Friar Laurence and The Nurse from Prokofiev's *Romeo and Juliet* are also useful (it is interesting to compare Prokofiev's Friar with Tchaikovsky's).

Once, I cheated and played some movements from *The Carnival of the Animals* without telling the children the title. Some of the results were very interesting.

I find *The Gramophone*, a monthly record reviewing magazine, very useful. Many excellent Bargain Label records are now available, and I think it is a good plan to buy cheap versions of the records one wants, wherever this is possible. For this, the Penguin *Guide to Bargain Classics* is invaluable. The Gramophone Classical Record Catalogue is published four times a year and lists all the currently available recordings with an index indicating prices. Their 'Recommended Recordings' can usefully supplement the Catalogue.

There are also a number of record libraries which regularly advertise in the record magazines. It is well worth investing in a record-playing system which has a cueing device which enables one to lower the stylus gently on to the record at any point which you select – with practice, it is possible to become very accurate indeed at this.

In conclusion, I must include a reminder that there are copyright laws covering the recording and reproduction of music.